Radical Revenge

Shame, Blame and the Urge for Retaliation

Radical Revenge

Shame, Blame and the Urge for Retaliation

Renée Danziger

a Free Association Books publication

First published by Free Association Books.

Copyright © 2021 Renée Danziger

A CIP Catalogue of this book is available from
the British Library

ISBN: 978-1-911-38347-5

Typeset by
Typo•glyphix
www.typoglyphix.co.uk

Cover design by Chandler Book Design

Printed and bound in England

This book is dedicated
to the memory of my parents,
Regina Liebermann Danziger
and
Leo Danziger

Contents

Acknowledgements

I'd like to thank all the many friends and colleagues who generously shared their thoughts about revenge with me over the past couple of years. I owe a special thanks to my sisters, Diana Danziger and Gloria Danziger, for their unfailing support and their very helpful comments on an earlier draft. Heartfelt thanks also to Emma Whitlock for her valuable feedback, which I appreciated enormously. I'm indebted to Kaye Wellings not only for commenting so helpfully on the draft but also for all the moral support she gave me along the way. Warm thanks to Jonathan Sklar for his invaluable insights, and to Ruth McCall for her thoughts on Chapter One. Stephen Frosh read a very preliminary outline and I'm grateful that he encouraged me to keep going. Peter Langman, who has conducted extensive research into school shootings in the US, gave me very good advice on gaining access to primary source materials. I'm particularly grateful to him for the excellent resources which he has made available on his website. Doing research on internet revenge proved to be more challenging than I'd expected, and I'd like to thank Kate Samuelson for the very useful pointers she gave me. I have so much to thank Jodie and Jon for, including their cheerful enthusiasm and continuing interest in my work on revenge. I'm also grateful to the many people I met at the Trump re-election rally in New Hampshire for talking so openly with me about their experiences and beliefs. A big thank you to Alice Solomons at Free Association Books, and to Lisa Findley for her very fine editing. Above all, my thanks to Neil Mitchell for supporting and spurring me on, commenting thoughtfully on each chapter, and restoring my confidence whenever it began to flag. For that, and for much more, I'm so very grateful.

Illustrations in this book are reproduced by kind permission as follows:

Peter Steiner *"On the Internet, nobody knows you're a dog"*: The New Yorker Cartoon Bank

Artemisia Gentileschi *Judith Beheading Holofernes*: Gallerie degli Uffizi, Florence, Italy 2020

Artemisia Gentileschi *Jael and Sisera*: Szépművészeti Múzeum, Museum of Fine Arts, Budapest, Hungary 2020

Artemisia Gentileschi *Self-Portrait as Saint Catherine of Alexandria*: National Gallery, London, UK 2020

Introduction

Pondering the punishment of French collaborators in 1946, Simone de Beauvoir hit upon a fundamental truth. "Vengeance is not justified by realistic considerations," she wrote. "To the contrary: if all we cared about was effectiveness, we'd renounce the urge to punish" (de Beauvoir 1946). She had a point. Revenge does nothing to undo the harms that have been done and it rarely brings more than a fleeting sense of satisfaction. Worse still, revenge often provokes counter-revenge, leading to a destructive cycle that can result in full-scale conflict. And yet, despite all this, most of us find it impossible to resist the urge for revenge. What makes this urge so compelling? And why can some people only satisfy it with extreme and destructive acts? These questions have a particular urgency at a time when social media offer new and brutal forms of revenge, and the rise of populism has brought angry calls for retribution against minorities and other perceived enemies. This book sets out a new way of thinking about our proclivity for revenge, and through the concept of *radical revenge* it gives some meaning to what may otherwise appear to be senseless acts of wanton destruction.

Revenge as a fact of life

Put simply, revenge consists of A retaliating against B in response to (the belief that) B has harmed A. Revenge is a form of aggression, but the two are not synonymous. Aggression can be mobilised for all sorts of reasons, including defence against a threatened or actual attack, whereas revenge is specifically about payback and is accompanied by a distinctive feeling of righteous redress.

It's no exaggeration to suggest that revenge has shaped human history. Over the centuries it has fuelled assassinations, executions, persecution, protests and bloody battles, from King Menelaus's revenge on the Trojans after Paris ran off with Helen; to the brutal punishment of alleged heretics during the Spanish Inquisition; to the attacks on individuals associated with the *ancien régime* during the French Revolution; the assassination of Archduke Franz Ferdinand in Sarajevo in 1914 and its bloody aftermath; the genocide in Rwanda in the early 1990s; and the ethnic cleansing in parts of the former Yugoslavia. In these, and in so many other conflicts around the world, the desire for revenge has played its part.

Revenge punctuates everyday life too, so much so that we may not even recognise it as revenge. Toddlers will happily play together until one of them snatches the other's toy; the aggrieved child responds by knocking down the first child's tower of bricks. School pupils enjoy spending time together until one hears that the other has achieved a better exam result, at which point they start to spread rumours that their rival is a boring swot. When someone cuts into a long queue of people waiting for the bus, the person behind them might make a point of pushing into them as they step onto the bus. A customer who complains that his food is cold might receive a warmer dish which has the waiter's saliva secretly stirred in to it. When a spouse is found to have been unfaithful, they may find their favourite jacket torn to shreds. Examples abound.

Despite our familiarity with revenge, it remains a constant source of fascination and a recurring theme in some of the world's greatest literature, from Euripides's *Medea* and Sophocles's *Electra*, to Shakespeare's *King Lear* and *Hamlet*, to Emily Brontë's *Wuthering Heights*, Nathaniel Hawthorne's *Scarlet Letter*, and Arthur Miller's *The Crucible*. Those who prefer watching rather than reading about revenge are spoiled for choice. They can switch on the US television series *Revenge* or the British mini-series *Retribution*; or they might prefer *The Sopranos*, *Billions*, *Succession* or *Damages*, each of which features plots and sub-plots laced with revenge. Cinema also explores revenge from a variety of angles, from Westerns about a lone cowboy seeking revenge on bandits, sheriffs, outlaws or Native Americans; to horror films such as Brian De Palma's *Carrie*; to violent dramas including *Death Wish*, *Kill Bill*, and of course Francis Ford Coppola's classic film, *The Godfather*. Who can forget the scene in which Jack Woltz wakes up to find the severed head of his prized race horse lying next to him in his bed? Distraught and dripping with the horse's blood, Woltz is forced to acknowledge that the Godfather will stop at nothing to punish those who defy him.

Clearly then, revenge is a central and often dramatic feature of our political, personal and cultural lives. Yet in most societies there is a persistent view that giving in to the urge for revenge is somehow unworthy[1]. For every dictum that tells us 'revenge is sweet' or 'don't get mad, get even', there is another aphorism advising us that 'an eye for an eye will make the whole world blind' and 'no revenge is more honourable than the one not taken'.

The negative normative value attached to revenge is reflected in, and bolstered by, religious teachings that include the Christian counsel to love your enemy and turn the other cheek, the Koran's repeated references to the need for forgiveness, and the Buddhist ideal of not holding on to ill will. Both the Old Testament (Leviticus) and the New Testament (Romans) warn similarly against taking revenge, commanding us to leave revenge in the hands of God[2].

There are also plenty of secular messages about the perils of revenge embedded in stories told to generations of children, from Aesop's *The Horse and the Stag* (in which the horse regrets having taken revenge on the stag because he ends up being enslaved by the humans who had helped him to wreak his revenge) to the Grimm brothers' *Snow White* (where the evil queen eventually gets her comeuppance for having taken revenge on Snow White for being so beautiful). Parents and teachers the world over have drawn on these sorts of cautionary tales in order to

---

1 Not all societies discourage revenge. Jon Elster amongst others has examined the profound social and cultural significance of revenge in blood feud societies (Elster 1990). Revenge plays a similarly important role in relationships within and between gangs. See Wright, Topalli and Jacques for a fascinating exposition of the relevance of retribution in gang dynamics (Wright et al 2017).

2 Elsewhere, the Old Testament advises us to take an eye for an eye, a tooth for a tooth, and a wound for a wound. This endorsement of talion is often misconstrued as encouragement to take revenge. Its aim is to *moderate* acts of revenge by ensuring that they are neither more lenient *nor more harmful* than the initial harm.

inculcate in their children a sense that revenge is both morally wrong and counter-productive. But mostly this is to no avail, and children – like adults – often give in to the urge for revenge when they feel they have been harmed.

What is it about the desire for revenge that makes it so difficult to give up? Many people attribute the ubiquity of revenge to its evolutionarily significant deterrent function (McCullough 2008; McCullough, Kurzban and Tabak 2013). The idea behind this is that, long ago, primitive man came to realise that if he hit back at his aggressor hard enough, the aggressor would refrain from any future attacks for fear of further payback. According to this view, revenge was an adaptive response to the perils of the state of nature, and it evolved over time to become a universal human trait.

Although the deterrence argument is in many ways convincing, experience shows that acts of revenge often provoke rather than deter further harms. The tragedy of Shakespeare's *Hamlet* lies not only in the Prince's tortured ambivalence about the meaning of his father's death and what it requires of him, but also in the revenge and counter-revenge killings that follow Hamlet's murder of Polonius. These sorts of cycles of revenge and counter-revenge are not only the stuff of theatre. They occur in everyday life (think for example of the tit-for-tat car hooting and aggressive driving that often precede acts of road rage), as well as in politics and warfare. The frequent attacks and counter-attacks between Israeli settlers and Palestinian inhabitants of the West Bank fundamentally concern the question of who rightfully owns the land but, in a more immediate sense, they are acts of revenge and counter-revenge for the killing of local people. On at least one occasion the word 'vengeance' was scribbled on dust-covered car windows to highlight what the West Bank shootings were about. Another tragic example is the Rwandan Hutus' slaughter of hundreds of thousands of Tutsis in revenge for the killing of President Habyarimana (and for decades of what was seen as unfair privilege), which then led to murderous counter-revenge attacks by Tutsi soldiers against those responsible for the genocide. There are unfortunately many other cases of revenge breeding counter-revenge which, taken together, suggest that revenge is as likely to escalate further violence as it is to deter it. It seems doubtful then that revenge would have evolved into a universal human trait simply because of its deterrent properties.

Nevertheless, the idea of deterrence is still widely used to explain – and to justify – acts of revenge. Four years prior to becoming President of the United States, Donald Trump spoke in support of what he regards as the deterrent function of revenge. While doing this he referred to another, possibly even more compelling, reason for taking revenge. In 2012 he said in a speech that if somebody hits you, you should hit them back five time harder. The reason for this, he said, was that "if they do that to you, you have to leave a tell-tale sign that they just can't take advantage of you. It's not so much for the person, *which does make you feel good*, to be honest with you, I've done it many times." (quoted in Corn 2016, my italics).

Trump mentions something here that many other people might be ashamed to admit to, namely that taking revenge makes you "feel good". If the pervasiveness of revenge can't be fully explained in terms of deterrence, maybe the explanation lies partly in the feel-good factor that Trump alludes to. Support for this idea is provided by a laboratory experiment carried out by Dominique de Quervain and his colleagues who used positron emission tomography (PET) scans to measure their subjects' neurological responses to the prospect of taking revenge against other participants in the experiment who had been found to abuse the subjects' trust. The study's findings strongly "support the hypothesis that people derive satisfaction from punishing norm violations" (de Quervain et al 2004).

But why should revenge be so pleasurable and gratifying? Some have argued that the satisfaction associated with revenge relates to the connection between revenge and honour, a connection perfectly embodied in the actions of Michelangelo Merisi da Caravaggio, the magnificent Italian baroque painter who lived from 1571 to 1610. Caravaggio adhered to a strict honour code which required him to exact retribution for any acts which he felt impugned his honour. When a Roman waiter questioned Caravaggio's taste, the artist smashed a plate into the waiter's mouth. When a young painter insulted Caravaggio behind his back, the young man was in turn attacked from behind with a sword. Caravaggio used his art to take revenge, too. One of his most majestic works, *The Conversion of St*

Paul, was painted in competition with a contemporary, Annibale Carracci, who painted the *Assumption of the Virgin*. The two paintings hang side-by-side in the Santa Maria del Popolo in Rome. A close look reveals what one critic refers to as Caravaggio's "vendetta mentality": the rump of St Paul's old carthorse faces Carracci's Madonna (Graham-Dixon 2010). This insult has been understood as Caravaggio's way of paying Carracci back for rivalling his greatness in the art world.

The philosopher Whitley Kaufman has argued cogently that revenge is ubiquitous because of its inextricable link with the defence of one's honour (Kaufman 2013). For Kaufman, revenge is not motivated by possible future benefits such as deterrence; rather, it is an act which in and of itself restores a person's honour. According to this view, it is the recovery of one's honour that makes revenge so compelling and so gratifying, whether it is carried out through spontaneous acts of payback or more carefully calculated acts of vengeance. The honour argument has the added benefit of accounting for the disturbing fact that in some cases people are willing to go to great lengths to take revenge, sometimes even risking their lives in order to get revenge in situations where life without honour does not feel worth living.

Although Kaufman's honour argument is a strong one, it does not account for the fact that the urge for revenge develops much earlier in life than notions of honour which are socially constructed. Unlike honour, the urge for revenge precedes socialisation and emerges in the very early stages of life, albeit in a very primitive form. Anyone who has watched a young baby engage in back-and-forth physical repartee with their mother or carer – sometimes more playfully, sometimes rather more crossly – will have seen a simple form of tit-for-tat going on between mother and baby. The renowned paediatrician and psychoanalyst Donald Winnicott found in his extensive experience with paediatric patients that a crude form of retaliation could even be observed in some babies just a few weeks old (Winnicott 1957). In other words, the urge for revenge emerges far earlier than our socialised thoughts and feelings about honour.

This is not to suggest that the baby conceives of its own actions in terms of revenge or retaliation. At this early stage it is an instinctive urge devoid of symbolic meaning for the infant who is as yet unable to think representationally. It is a primitive response to what feels like a threat to the physical self. But as the baby develops into a child and then an adult, the self acquires a multiplicity of physical, emotional and psychological features; threats to the self correspondingly become far more complex and nuanced. It is in these more mature stages of psychological and social development that a sense of shame and of honour come into play, often – but not always – triggering the urge for revenge as a means of restoring the sense of self. As this book shows, what can feel like an existential threat to one person's sense of self may feel like a relatively trivial slight to another. The difference in how harms are experienced, and whether they provoke an urge for revenge, arise out of the distinctive environments and relationships that shape each person from their earliest days onwards.

Seen in this light, the urge for revenge can be understood as a self-preservative urge. The easiest way to illustrate this is in counterfactual terms. Imagine a person – whether child or adult – who feels unjustly attacked in some way and who remains entirely devoid of any urge to retaliate in any way whatsoever. A person who blankly tolerates every offence, every harm and every threat and then simply walks away without any fantasy or desire for revenge would seem to be a broken person. By contrast, the person who wishes to protect and preserve his sense of self will look for a way to show himself (and others) that the aggressor has not prevailed. As I explain below, this can be done in all sorts of ways, some more harmful than others. What is important to note is that, although the urge for revenge is a universal, whether and how that urge is acted upon will vary from case to case.

The notion that revenge is about self-preservation could be objected to on the grounds that revenge is sometimes taken in the full knowledge that it will cost the avenger their life. That can hardly be considered an act of self-preservation. Or can it? It may not save the person's physical life, but it helps to preserve an essential sense of self-respect, and an inner sense of rightness for the shortened duration of their life. In Homer's *Iliad*, Achilles knew full well that avenging his beloved Patroclus's death would cost him his life. His mother, the sea nymph Thetis, had warned him this would happen, but despite this he went ahead and took his revenge by killing and dishonouring Hector, because otherwise life simply would not have been worth living.

The life-and-death importance of revenge takes on a slightly different hue in blood feud societies where vendettas between families or clans are often carried out over many years, often passing from one generation to the next. In a remarkable novel about a society dominated by blood feuds, the Albanian writer Ismael Kadare describes the powerful internal and external pressures that drive individuals to perpetuate vendettas. The protagonist of *Broken April* is Gjorg, a young man whose brother has been murdered. Gjorg is fully aware that tradition and honour require him to avenge his brother's death by killing the murderer. Failing to do this would mean losing the respect of his father, his family and his community. Yet at the same time, he knows that taking revenge on his brother's killer will oblige the rival family to reciprocate by killing him. According to society's unwritten rules, after avenging his brother's death, Gjorg will be granted just thirty days of safety before becoming the target of his opponent's revenge. The poignant conflict between needing to do the right thing by his community (which will lead to his own death), and young Gjorg's deep desire for life, is at the heart of this tragic novel.

What is clear from Gjorg's story is his belief that life would become unbearable if he were to resist the social pressures that demand acts of revenge, even though bowing to those pressures leads to certain death (Elster 1990). A similar dynamic operates in many street gang cultures, where young men willingly risk serious injury and even death in order to retaliate against rival gang members (Wright et al 2017). Revenge in these cases is about preserving an inner sense of self – which includes a sense of honour – for however long one remains alive, even though it means significantly shortening one's life.

Revenge is not always enacted in such dramatic ways. In fact, often the urge for revenge can be quelled with a vivid *fantasy*, rather than through action. The fantasy may be fleeting and fairly simple, like imagining setting off a stink bomb at a noisy neighbour's doorstep, or punching a bullying boss in the face. Or it might be more elaborate, involving ideas of blackmail, torture or murder. Fortunately, most of us stop short of acting out these sorts of fantasies, for reasons both of principle and pragmatism.

Sometimes the urge to punish an enemy is displaced onto an inanimate object. An obvious example would be voodoo dolls, but displaced revenge is also common among young children who can sometimes be seen smacking their teddy bears or tearing off the heads of dolls whilst imagining (not always consciously) that the toy is the person whom they feel has harmed them in some way. In this way the child the can satisfy two conflicting wishes: on the one hand, a desire to punish the offending person, and on the other hand, a need to protect that person (and themselves) from their destructive wishes. George Eliot's *Mill on the Floss* comes to mind where the young Maggie Tulliver drives nails into the head of a large wooden doll which, for Maggie, represents the much-hated Aunt Glegg.

The usefulness of fantasy for discharging the urge for revenge was noted by Sigmund Freud who was intrigued by the game his one-and-a-half-year-old grandson invented. One day, when the little boy's mother had gone out, Freud watched his grandson playing with a wooden reel which had a string attached to it. Holding the end of the string in his hand, the boy repeatedly threw the reel over the edge of his cot to make it disappear, then made it reappear by pulling up the string. As the reel disappeared, the boy said "fort" (German for 'gone'); as it reappeared, he said "da" (there). The meaning of the fort-da game is open to interpretation. Freud understood it primarily as a means by which the child could feel a sense of mastery by making the reel disappear and reappear and, in this way, through fantasy, he could recover from having passively to accept the absence of his mother. But, Freud adds, there is another way to think about the fort-da game, namely:

> Throwing away the object so that it was 'gone' might satisfy an impulse of the child's, which was suppressed in his actual life, to revenge himself on his mother for going away from him. In that case it would have a defiant meaning: 'All right, then, go away! I don't need you. I'm sending you away myself.' (Freud 1920)

These sorts of fantasied expressions of revenge enable the person to avenge themselves without actually causing undue harm to others. But in many cases fantasied revenge is not enough, and the urge for revenge has to be enacted in a more direct way. Sometimes the revenge taken is fairly ordinary but, as this book will show, often the enactment of revenge is more destructive than the original harm would seem to warrant. These are the cases which grab our attention, where the acts of revenge are brutal, relentless and – for many of us – difficult to comprehend. This book is an attempt to explain what lies behind some of these more extreme acts of revenge – what I refer to as radical revenge.

About this book

My fascination with revenge is linked partly to my personal history. As I explain in Chapter Five, both of my parents were survivors of the Shoah. I'm not sure how old I was when I first became aware of this fact, but I do remember thinking for a while that my mother and father must have been very naughty at school to have been sent to a summer camp where they had to spend all their time learning to concentrate. Gradually it dawned on me that being sent to a concentration camp wasn't a punishment for naughtiness, but – even more confusingly – it was a punishment for being Jewish! This seemed crazy and unfair to me, all the more so when I found out what concentration camps actually were. Growing up in the 1960s and '70s, I knew that many concentration camp survivors and their families had taken a mostly symbolic sort of revenge for their suffering by boycotting German goods and refusing to set foot in Germany or Austria. But my parents didn't seem to bother with revenge. They didn't mind whether their car or fridge was made in Germany or anywhere else. Not only that, but in 1966 they moved our family from the US back to Germany, where we lived for a number of years. For a long time I wondered why my parents didn't want some sort of revenge, even some token payback, for the appalling losses and unimaginable suffering that I knew they had endured.

Very slowly, I came to see things differently. Although my family has always lived in the shadow of the Shoah, my parents managed over the years to build a good enough life for us. They – we – were able to live, to laugh and, most importantly, to love. It took me a long time, and many years of psychoanalysis with a very wise analyst, to work out that living a good enough life was quite possibly the best revenge of all on those who had tried to reduce my parents, quite literally, to nothingness.

In trying to understand the many dimensions of revenge, I've been fortunate to be able to draw on my work as a psychoanalyst. I haven't referred directly to any past or present patients, but the many insights that they've shared with me have helped me to think about some of the complex and painful feelings associated with revenge. I've also made use of the rich psychoanalytic literature on trauma, shame, envy and narcissism, all of which come into play in most acts of radical revenge. I should stress though that while I make extensive use of psychoanalytic theories and concepts, my aim in this book is to discuss these ideas in ways that don't assume a familiarity with the psychoanalytic literature.

In Chapter One I introduce my concept of radical revenge and propose that revenge can be thought of in terms of a continuum with retributive justice at one end, radical revenge at the other, and what I call ordinary revenge somewhere in the middle. The chapter goes on to examine why some people can only satisfy their urge for revenge through extreme and destructive acts. It also highlights the paradoxical relationship between shame and revenge. While on the one hand feelings of shame frequently give rise to an irresistible urge for revenge, on the other hand, shame often helps to temper acts of revenge, where people feel too ashamed to enact the radical revenge that they secretly wish for.

Chapters Two, Three and Four apply these ideas about shame and revenge to specific cases of radical revenge. Chapter Two is concerned with mass shootings in the US. Drawing as far as possible on primary source material, this chapter tells the stories of three different mass shooters and shows how in each case the shooter's mind was overwhelmed by an urge for revenge arising out of unbearable feelings of grievance, shame and envy. From the outsider's point of view, the shootings were wanton acts of violence and destruction; from the shooters' points of view, they were necessary acts of radical revenge.

Introduction

Chapter Three considers how our primordial urge for revenge fits in with the modern world of internet technology. Focussing on revenge porn, trolling and swatting, the chapter looks at what happens when revenge seekers believe that they cannot be seen, identified or shamed by their actions. The evidence suggests that feelings of invisibility and unaccountability lead to a significant increase in the incidence and the destructiveness of acts of radical revenge. The cases that are discussed in both Chapters Two and Three point to a significant gender imbalance among perpetrators of radical revenge, so Chapter Three concludes with some thoughts about the links between gender, misogyny and radical revenge. Whether my findings about gender and radical revenge are generalisable will require more research, but they did at least help me to decide which pronouns to use in this book. Although I was reluctant to perpetuate gendered stereotypes and inequalities by referring to significant actors as 'he', I felt that using 'she' to refer to perpetrators of radical revenge would not be in keeping with the material in this book. With this in mind, I decided to use 'he' when discussing in general terms the perpetrators of radical revenge.

Chapter Four looks at groups and radical revenge. It begins by considering why individuals may be more likely to resort to radical revenge when they are members of a group, paying particular attention to the significance of group identity, the reduced sense of individual accountability, and the role that leaders can play in fomenting a group's desire for radical revenge. The chapter then focuses on the dynamic between President Trump and his followers in the development of a systematic programme of radical revenge against Blacks, Hispanics and other minorities which were blamed for social and economic difficulties that they did not in fact cause.

Chapter Five moves away from radical revenge and turns instead to thoughts about radically different ways of taking revenge. This chapter tells the stories of four remarkable individuals who suffered exceptionally cruel and inhumane treatment, and describes how they were each able to find creative and life-affirming ways to satisfy their need for revenge.

Finally, Chapter Six pulls together the main findings of this book, and concludes with some thoughts about the likely impact of the trend towards a post-truth culture on acts of revenge. The book ends with an unanswered question: as the line between what is real and what is fake becomes ever more blurred, might we all become more prone to take radical revenge unwittingly against people who are not in reality responsible for our grievances?

Inevitably there are aspects of revenge which are not discussed in this book. Probably the single greatest omission is a consideration of what revenge means and what it can look like in different cultures and sub-cultures. A comparative study of revenge would be fascinating, but is unfortunately beyond the scope of this book. My focus here has been chiefly on cases of radical revenge in the US and Britain. I chose to look at mass shootings – which are radical acts by any standards – in order to investigate the explanatory value of the concept of radical revenge. It felt especially important to look at cyber revenge partly because of the dramatic increase in both the incidence and the significance of this sort of revenge in recent years, and also because it provides such a good counterfactual for understanding the role that shame can play in *inhibiting* acts of revenge. While mass shootings and cyber revenge are about the actions of aggrieved individuals, it seemed essential also to give some thought to revenge at the group level. Writing this book at a time when populism is gaining ground not only in the US and UK, but around the world from Brazil to the Philippines, and from Italy to India, it seemed imperative to explore the role of radical revenge in groups, and in particular the importance of revenge in strengthening the relationship between demagogues and their followers.

Although much of the material presented here is dark and disturbing, what I hope also comes across in the following chapters is that, although we cannot purge ourselves of the desire for revenge, there is much to be gained by reflecting on whether, when and how we want to act on that desire.

Chapter One
Radical Revenge

Writing in the seventeenth century, the English philosopher Thomas Hobbes famously described life in an imagined state of nature as being solitary, poor, nasty, brutish and short. Believing that people would willingly give up the freedoms of the state of nature in exchange for a less precarious life, Hobbes hypothesised that human society is based on a social contract through which individuals relinquish their autonomy and authorise a central governing body to establish and enforce rules to ensure that life is safe and sound. A similar sort of paradigm applies to revenge. With one eye on security and stability, we give up our right to avenge ourselves at will and instead authorise lawyers to argue our case and judges to mete out punishments according to a clearly defined system of retributive justice.

While the justice system offers a regulated process for prosecution and punishment, the law clearly does not, and often cannot, cover all areas of conflict. In these extra-judicial cases, revenge is left in the hands of the individuals concerned. Although revenge is sometimes violent, dramatic and bloody, in most cases it is relatively pedestrian, and sometimes so trivial that the individual does not even think of their retaliatory actions as revenge. For the purposes of this study, however, all acts of retaliation are regarded as acts of revenge, so this chapter begins by setting out some criteria with which to distinguish reasonable or ordinary acts of revenge from something altogether more dangerous and troubling.

Revenge on a continuum

One way to think about revenge is in terms of the continuum shown in Figure 1. At one end lies retributive justice where major acts of revenge are taken out of the hands of the aggrieved and delegated to those who are authorised to determine and oversee appropriate punishments for individuals found guilty of specific crimes. Where the law is not involved in the punishment, the aggrieved person might take comfort in a revenge fantasy, or he might be inclined to enact some sort of revenge. The revenge he takes is 'ordinary' to the extent that it meets the criteria of proportionality, intentionality and culpability, each of which is discussed below. As Figure 1 indicates, the less an act of revenge meets these criteria, the more radical it is. At the far end of the continuum are the most radical acts of revenge which appear to take no account of proportionality, intentionality or culpability.

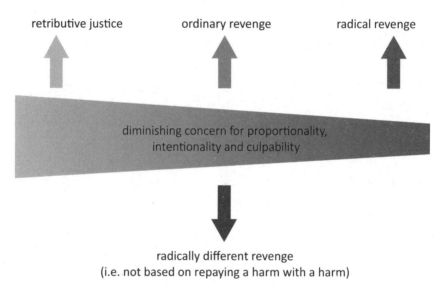

FIGURE 1 : REVENGE ON A CONTINUUM

Most acts of revenge aim to restore a damaged sense of self by repaying a (perceived) harm with another harm in order to demonstrate that the aggressor has not prevailed. As Figure 1 indicates, there can also be acts of radically different revenge defined as such because, instead of repaying a harm with a harm, these acts aim to restore the damaged sense of self through creative and life-affirming measures. This idea will be explored in detail in Chapter Five.

Radical Revenge

In his review of psychoanalytic work on revenge, Salman Akhtar develops a concept of 'good enough revenge' which provides a useful starting point for thinking about what constitutes an act of ordinary revenge. One of Akhtar's key criteria for good enough revenge is that it consists of relatively straightforward, single-act responses to specific harms rather than arising out of a persistent sense of grievance and an insatiable desire for retaliation (Akhtar 2014). This is an important distinction and is in keeping with the contrast Karen Horney draws between isolated acts of angry revenge on the one hand, and what she calls compulsive vindictiveness on the other (Horney 1948).

However, being a one-off act of retaliation for a specific harm is not in and of itself sufficient to qualify as ordinary revenge. It does not seem ordinary, for instance, to commit murder as a one-off response to a verbal insult. Ordinary acts of revenge therefore not only have to be one-off; they also have to be *proportionate* to the offence caused.

It could be objected that upholding talion, or the principle of proportionality, as the basis for ordinary revenge is in effect to condone a cycle of violence in which murder is repaid with murder, and destruction with destruction. The response to this objection would be that although proportionality is a necessary criterion for ordinary revenge, it is not sufficient. Firstly, in the case of grave harms (such as murder) that fall under the jurisdiction of the legal system, the principles and practice of retributive justice, rather than individual revenge, form the basis of appropriate retribution. Secondly, in cases that fall outside the justice system, there are two further conditions that must be met for revenge to be considered reasonable and ordinary. These relate to the criteria of intentionality and culpability. To meet the intentionality requirement, the revenge seeker has to be reasonably certain that the person who harmed him actually *intended* to do so. To meet the culpability requirement, the revenge seeker must direct the act of revenge at whoever has in reality caused the harm (whether intentionally or not).

Turning first to the criterion of intentionality, this is at first sight relatively easy to understand. The idea behind it is formulated by the philosopher P.F. Strawson, who writes: "If someone treads on my hand accidentally, while trying to help me, the pain may be no less acute than if he treads on it in contemptuous disregard of my existence or with the malevolent wish to injure me. But I shall generally feel in the second case a kind and degree of resentment that I shall not feel in the first" (Strawson 1974, p.6). Strawson's distinction is crucial to thoughts about revenge. It would be unreasonable for him to take revenge against the person who accidentally steps on his hand while trying to help him, but understandable if he wanted to retaliate against the person who has malevolent wishes to injure him. What a psychoanalytic perspective can add to this is that if the person whose hand is stepped on is so overwhelmed by pre-existing grievance that he is continually resentful, or if he is susceptible to paranoid thoughts and permanently mistrustful of the intentions of others, he may not be able to make this critical distinction between intentional and unintentional harm. He might feel so deeply resentful and/or so paranoid that he will be gripped by an urge for revenge *regardless* of the actual intentions of the person who stepped on his hand. This would be an example of radical revenge. By contrast, ordinary revenge presumes the ability to make the distinction between intended and unintended harms, and to act accordingly.

The culpability criterion is equally important for distinguishing ordinary revenge from something which is more radical. Put very simply, ordinary revenge is aimed at the person who has actually harmed you, whereas radical revenge can be aimed at someone who has not *in reality* caused you any harm at all. For example, beating a wife in unconscious revenge against what may have been a depriving mother or a violent and humiliating father in earlier life would not meet the culpability requirement. As psychoanalysis shows, however, causal culpability is not always easy to pinpoint. This can make it difficult to define with precision whether a particular act is ordinary revenge or something more troubling. Take the following hypothetical example. Arthur and Ben are working together on a project. Arthur asks Ben a foolish question about the work they are engaged in, and Ben laughs disparagingly at Arthur's ignorance. Feeling humiliated by Ben's laughter, Arthur punches Ben in the face. It could be argued that Ben is culpable because he hurt Arthur's feelings through his contemptuous laughter. But how much weight should we give to the fact that Arthur had grown up with parents who regularly demeaned him in favour of his younger and smarter sibling? Is Arthur simply responding to Ben's disdain when he punches him? Or is he in fact responding to an unconscious re-living of earlier experiences of unbearable shame? Or is it a bit of both? This sort of ambiguity, arising out of the rich and layered nature of the unconscious, makes the attribution of culpability – in psychoanalytic if not legal terms – deeply problematic. It is not always easy to distinguish ordinary from radical revenge, which is why thinking in terms of a continuum can be helpful.

Shame and Envy

In the above example, Arthur reacts to his feelings of shame and humiliation by punching Ben in the face. One way of explaining this act of radical revenge is to say that Ben's contempt caused Arthur such a deep narcissistic wound that it shook his sense of self, and in that moment he felt compelled to relieve himself of his pain and shame by making Ben the one to feel weak, vulnerable and shamed instead.

Shame is often at the heart of acts of revenge because of the way it can shake or damage a person's sense of self. Shame arises out of feeling exposed as being weak, inept, cowardly or otherwise wanting. Being shown up in this way makes a person feel pitiful, contemptible and even worthless. This is a doubly difficult experience because the exposure takes place at two levels: in the eyes of others, and also in terms of one's own self-regard.

Most people know what it is like to feel shame in the eyes of others. It is at best an uncomfortable and at worst a deeply troubling, sometimes even overwhelming, experience. But importantly, being shamed in front of others does not always result in acts of retaliation; sometimes it is possible to recover from shame without resorting to acts of revenge. Donald Campbell's concept of a shame shield is useful for understanding how recovery from a shameful experience is possible (Campbell 1994). Campbell points out that someone who feels ashamed may reflexively bring their hands up to cover their face, thereby expressing quite concretely the need we all have to shield ourselves from further exposure and the deepening shame that this would bring. There are other ways of hiding including keeping quiet, pretending that one is not shamed at all, or withdrawing from public view for a given period of time. Even blushing could be thought of as a primitive form of signalling to others to avert their gaze for a short while. All of these different forms of hiding one's shame serve a dual purpose: they help to avoid the deepening shame brought about by a continued sense of exposure to others; and in doing so they provide the person with sufficient time and space to come to terms in their own minds with whatever has shamed them. Under these conditions, the need to enact some form of revenge can recede, as more measured thinking takes its place. By contrast, when the shame shield is violated – in other words, when others do not respect the shamed person's need to protect themselves from further exposure and shame – the ego can feel overwhelmed by the continuing experience of shame, resulting in a destabilising experience of loss of self-regard and sense of self. In these cases, the person needs to find other ways to defend himself. One way is by projecting the feelings of shame onto others.

Campbell describes this process of projection in the context of child sexual abuse. He describes how the abused child's feelings of shame, confusion and self-disgust are often carried by the child into adulthood. How can a person cope when they are racked by so much inner pain? Depending on the circumstances, they might try to numb the pain with drugs and alcohol; or they might live with severe anxiety, panic attacks and an inner torment that they struggle to contain; or they might develop various physical symptoms that express their psychic pain. And then there are the cases that Campbell discusses, where the adult feels that the only way he can function is by projecting his difficult feelings onto someone else. One way of doing this is by abusing another child and making *them* the one who feels shamed, confused and defiled. As Campbell says, "In this way, the abused child becomes the abuser".

The problem with fending off shame and other difficult feelings by projecting them onto others is that this can only provide the person with temporary relief. Projection is based on what Thomas Ogden calls 'magical thinking', the purpose of which is to evade what is often a painful truth about one's internal and external life (Ogden 2010). But sooner or later, the truth comes back into focus. For instance, in the example discussed earlier, Arthur may have felt a moment of satisfaction when he punched Ben in revenge for Ben shaming him, but given Arthur's underlying (perhaps unconscious) sense of inferiority and grievance, it would only be a matter of time before someone or something else aroused his feeling of being shamefully inadequate. In Campbell's example, the adult survivor of child abuse may get passing relief by projecting feelings of shame and self-disgust onto another abused child, but this relief does not last, a fact which goes some way to explaining why many child abusers are repeat offenders.

Campbell's concept of the shame shield helps to understand the dynamic between shame and revenge. Take the following case. In October 2018 the press reported that the mother of a fourteen-year-old boy had called the police to her home in south Wales after her son had allegedly attacked her. One of the two police officers who arrived at the house was a fifty-year-old male officer who specialised in hate crimes. He found the boy had locked himself in the bathroom. The police officer forced his way in and allegedly thrust his arm across the throat of the boy who then called the policemen "pigs". The police officer grabbed the boy's phone but was unable to switch it off, at which point the boy called him a "pussy". The police officer then punched the boy and, telling the boy he was doing his mother a favour, he punched him in the face twice more.

The police officer's shame at fumbling and failing to switch off the boy's phone might have been just about bearable if he could have somehow saved face but instead of being given this opportunity, his shame shield was breached when the boy mocked him by calling him a pussy. The police officer's sense of self became so injured that punching the boy may have felt in that moment like the only immediate means of recovery, as it enabled the police officer to project the vulnerability and feelings of shame onto the boy.

In this example the policeman's act of revenge could be considered radical in so far as it was unarguably disproportionate to the boy's offence.

Being called pig or pussy does not warrant punching a fourteen-year-old child under any circumstances. While the policeman's actions were neither reasonable nor ordinary, they can be more easily understood when framed in the context of the policeman's deep sense of shame, and his inability to recover from this before resorting to violence.

Shame is not only about exposure in the eyes of others; it is also a feeling of having let oneself down, of being exposed as inadequate or contemptible "under the glare of one's own mind's eye" (Wurmser 2015). In psychoanalytic terms, the mind's eye can be thought of as the *ego ideal*, a concept which Charles Rycroft helpfully describes as "the self's conception of how he wishes to be" (Rycroft 1968). How we wish to be is in turn based on internal representations of our parent figures as well as later people who have deeply influenced our sense of how we want ourselves to be. We may not be conscious day-to-day of the influence that our ego ideal has on our thoughts and behaviours, but it quietly shapes and defines our expectations of ourselves throughout our lives. When we feel we have approximated these expectations we may experience a sense of inner well-being; on the other hand, when we fail to do so there can be can be a sense of inadequacy or failure, and terrible shame resulting from the judgements of the superego.

This inner sense of failure and shame can be profoundly disturbing. It can arise from something someone else says or does (for instance Ben's contemptuous reply to Arthur's foolish question, or the boy taunting the policeman), or it can result from feeling that one has less, or is lesser, than someone else. Whether or not the feeling of being lesser is grounded in reality, it can give rise to a persistent sense of grievance and a vengeful envy of those who seem to have whatever is felt to be lacking.

Psychoanalysts differ sharply in their views of when the experience of envy first develops. Those who share Melanie Klein's view generally regard the new-born infant as being filled with a destructive envy of the mother's breast and of the goodness and creativity which it represents. Where the mother is unable to tolerate and take in the infant's powerfully envious feelings and transform them into something less frightening and more manageable for the infant, this can lead to later emotional and psychological problems. Conversely, Donald Winnicott cautioned against imputing emotions from a later stage of development onto young infants. Although a baby at the breast may appear to be aggressively attacking the mother, for Winnicott this is not about an envious desire to destroy the breast, but rather an expression of what he calls 'mouth love'. The pain it may cause to the mother is inflicted by chance, not by intention (Winnicott 1939). Notwithstanding these disagreements about the origins of envy and their profound implications for understanding the human spirit, there is a wide consensus on the potential destructiveness of envious feelings. Deep and persistent envy may flood a person with feelings of resentment which in turn can give rise to an irresistible urge to take radical revenge on those who appear to be unfairly better off, even though these people may not have intentionally done anything to cause harm to the revenge taker.

Leonard Shengold makes a helpful distinction between ordinary envy which is about wanting what someone else has (what some might call jealousy), and malignant envy which arises from a feeling that the other person has something which should rightfully belong to you (Shengold 1994). Malignant envy has a delusional quality in so far as it is based on an unconscious fantasy that what the other person has or is, was somehow taken away from oneself. Shengold argues that malignant envy is often associated with earlier experiences of having been emotionally deprived, an important idea which will be returned to later in this chapter. Acknowledging this link between harms suffered in early life, and destructive feelings that may be aroused later when the person is confronted by experiences associated in some way with their earlier suffering, makes it easier to understand why an individual might want to take revenge against someone who may not have intended to harm them.

So far, this chapter has argued that shaming experiences can threaten a person's sense of self, which in turn provokes an urge for revenge. But this is not the only significance that shame has for revenge. While on the one hand feelings of shame can spark the urge for revenge, on the other hand the fear of being shamed by transgressing social norms may stop an aggrieved person from giving in to an urge for extreme or radical revenge.

Someone who has been hurt and shamed might fantasise about destroying the aggressor, but they usually refrain from acting on their destructive fantasies, at least in part because of the (conscious or unconscious) fear of social disapprobation, and the shame that this would bring[3]. Society's norms regarding what is and is not reasonable behaviour, and the fear of being shamed by acting outside the tramlines of these norms, are key factors in holding back a person who might *wish* for radical revenge, but who will settle for something more ordinary. The significance of the regulating function of shame is underlined in later chapters which show that, when a person believes that he has eluded both the gaze of others and of his own inner eye, he is more inclined to act shamelessly on his urge for radical revenge.

The pull towards radical revenge

Although the fear of shame often functions as a moderating force, sometimes the urge for radical revenge is so strong that it overrides any sense of shame. In these cases, people will be much more inclined to act on their urge for radical revenge. There are at least four factors that can intensify the pull towards radical revenge. These are: (i) deprivation and despair; (ii) the thin-skinned narcissist's sensitivity to slights and insults; (iii) a vindictive personality; and (iv) a pathological mistrust of the motives and behaviour of others. Although each of these features is discussed separately below, in practice they often co-exist, making the urge for radical revenge all the more difficult to resist.

(i) Deprivation and despair

Clinical studies have shown that early trauma can lead to a sense of hopelessness and deep despair in later life (Bowlby 1944; Rosenfeld 1987; Sklar 2011; Socarides 1966; Winnicott 1958). These feelings are difficult to

---

3   In a footnote in *Civilization and its Discontents*, Freud refers to the very early civilising influence of shame as he speculates that when primitive man assumed an upright gait, he would have been shamed by the exposure of his genitals which had previously been concealed and protected. And so, writes Freud, "the fateful process of civilization would have thus set in with man's adoption of an erect posture" (Freud 1930).

bear, and often need to be defended against in order for the person to feel able to continue functioning. Defences vary from person to person. One person might express their pain and anger psycho-somatically, while another might develop an over-confident and brash manner of being so as to avoid the pain of their inner hopelessness. Another way of defending against this psychic pain is by projecting it onto others, which is a key component of revenge. However, as mentioned earlier, while projection may feel gratifying in one-off cases of ordinary revenge, in cases of radical revenge which often spring from deep-rooted and complex feelings of despair and anger, the projection only provides fleeting relief, because the familiar feelings of despair and hopelessness will soon return.

The term *trauma* is a broad one, and can relate to experiences of sexual, physical or emotional abuse, or terrible losses such as the early death of a parent, or from witnessing something so horrific that the experience cannot be processed. Trauma can also result from more or less consistent privation or deprivation in early life. Early (de)privation in this context refers to the (de)privation experienced by a baby and growing child whose primary carer cannot meet their emotional and developmental needs in a more or less consistent way. It is important to stress that the concept of cumulative trauma does not refer to situations where a mother (or other primary carer) sometimes fails to respond to the psychological or physical needs of her baby. These occasions are not only inevitable; they are essential for the baby's healthy development towards greater independence. But when the mother/carer is repeatedly and regularly unable to protect and provide for the baby's needs, the effect is cumulatively traumatic. Being cumulative, its consequences only become fully apparent in later life (Khan 1963).

The links that can sometimes develop between cumulative trauma, mental distress and an increased tendency towards vengefulness were highlighted by Charles Socarides who observed that many of his patients who had seemed especially vengeful had in fact suffered an early life of privation which had led to an inability to bear any deprivation in later life (Socarides 1966). Robert Lane similarly found that the desire for revenge is rooted in '"early mismatches between mother and infant", suggesting that where the mother is unable to respond to her child's need for comfort and care, the child can easily become frustrated and vengeful (Lane 1995). A poignant example of emotional deprivation leading to anti-social behaviour is given by the psychoanalyst and psychiatrist John Bowlby in his study of forty-four juvenile thieves (Bowlby 1944). In this study, Bowlby highlighted the link between maternal deprivation and later criminal behaviour. He compared forty-four juvenile thieves with forty-four adolescents who did not steal despite having had emotional problems. What he found was that fourteen of the children in the thieves group were what he called 'affectionless', by which he meant they appeared to be incapable of affection. In contrast to this, none of the children in the control group of adolescents were affectionless. He also found that seventeen of the youngsters in the thieves group had been separated from their mothers for more than six months before the age of five, as compared with only two children in the control group. From these findings Bowlby suggested there was a correlation between maternal deprivation in infancy and subsequent criminal behaviour in adolescence.

For Bowlby, these findings had a direct bearing on the urge for vengeance. As he put it, "If one has suffered great deprivation oneself, one will feel inclined to inflict equal suffering on someone else" (Bowlby 1944, p.122). He described the experience of one of the children in his study who had explained that his stealing was often motivated by revenge. This child described his feelings of resentment towards his younger brother whom he felt had had all of his mother's attention and love. He resorted to stealing partly in order to provide himself with material goods to make up for what he felt he was missing out on, but also to take revenge on his mother who had admitted that she preferred the younger son. The child remembered that he often went out stealing from others shortly after his mother had shouted at him or punished him. This provides a poignant example of revenge that does not take account of culpability, as the people he stole from were not in reality the people who had harmed him.

Trauma and deprivation can understandably contribute to feelings of despair and envy. There are all sorts of ways of defending against these feelings, one of which is to develop a conviction that someone must pay for one's suffering. When the despairing person takes revenge against a teacher, a colleague, or a lover (who have not in reality caused any harm), these people do not merely *represent* their depriving parents; in the perpetrator's unconscious mind, in that moment of revenge-taking, they *are* the depriving parents. In other words, the feelings engendered by very early relationships are transferred unconsciously onto later relationships. This idea of the transfer of feelings from early relationships onto later ones, which was first described by Freud in 1895, helps us to understand why revenge is sometimes so extreme, and why it is sometimes targeted at people who may not *in reality* have harmed the avenger at all.

(ii) The sensitivities of the thin-skinned narcissist
Although shame is often at the root of the urge for revenge, not everyone experiences a shaming situation in the same way. What for one person is an uncomfortable moment could for someone else be an experience of excruciating humiliation. Much will depend on the person's emotional and psychological make-up which, as explained above, evolves to a great extent out of their earlier experiences.

Take the following hypothetical example. Fred and George are having a drink in their local pub. They have come straight from their work as doormen at a nearby hotel, and are still wearing their rather gaudy, gold-buttoned uniforms. As they chat, they become aware that the men at the next table are looking at them and laughing. Fred and George hear the other men making rude comments about their clothes and their appearance. Fred swears at the men. George walks over to where the men are sitting, and kicks them both to the ground. As the men try to defend themselves, George threatens to kill them if they say anything more about George or Fred. Fred's reaction was one-off and relatively proportionate. George's extreme response suggests a very fragile sense of self: a self that is easily hurt, shamed and shaken. George may well be what is known as a 'thin-skinned narcissist'.

The idea of thin-skinned narcissism was first elaborated by Herbert Rosenfeld who applied the concept to people who (like the hypothetical George) are hypersensitive and easily hurt, and who find shame unbearably difficult (Rosenfeld 1987). Like other thin-skinned narcissists, George will have found ways to defend against these painful feelings. But the shame shield of thin-skinned narcissists is usually very brittle, and easily punctured. When this happens, further defences against shame may be needed, including the projection of intolerable shame feelings onto others. In an important and influential contribution to the subject of narcissism, Rosenfeld explains that in his clinical experience,

> 'thin-skinned' narcissistic patients were, as children, repeatedly severely *traumatized in their feelings of self-regard*. They seem to have *felt persistently and excessively inferior, ashamed and vulnerable, and rejected by everybody*. During puberty and later on, through their intellectual capacities and physical prowess, they often succeeded if not in overcoming at least in hiding their sense of inferiority, and thus often gained recognition and success in life... there is a great deal of over-compensation and a tendency to feel superior in certain areas, with the result that the patient's sense of triumph and revenge against the parents or siblings (by whom he felt so belittled and humiliated) has been stimulated... (Rosenfeld 1987, p.274–5, *my italics*)

This highlights the likely links between early experiences of shame and trauma, feelings of hopelessness, and the subsequent development of narcissistic defences to compensate for the later inability to tolerate shame.

It is important to acknowledge that not everyone who is susceptible to intense feelings of shame and envy manages these feelings through acts of radical revenge. Some people try to control their feelings by denying them altogether, for instance by convincing themselves that they simply do not care what other people think of them. Piers and Singer suggest another way of dealing with overwhelming shame is through "a peculiar narcissistic maneuver [sic] that prevents the defeat from being inflicted by others by bringing it about oneself". In other words, where the anticipatory anxiety of being shamed is so intense, a certain type of person will pre-empt being shamed by others by bringing the shame onto themselves first so that they can say 'nobody did this to me, I did it to myself' (Piers and Singer 1953).

(iii) The vindictive personality

People with a deep and fixed sense of grievance often develop a vengeful way of relating to others. Karen Horney called this the 'vindictive personality' which she described as being driven by an obsessive desire to denigrate and humiliate others so as to achieve a feeling of triumph over them (Horney 1948). Wilhelm Reich's concept of character armour is helpful for understanding why qualities such as spite and vindictiveness might pervade a personality. The idea behind character armour is that many of us unconsciously defend ourselves against our unwanted inclinations and impulses by adopting a particular way of being, or character, that keeps these disturbing impulses and urges at bay. Examples of this could include relating to others in an overly submissive and self-deprecating fashion so as to defend against hostile and aggressive feelings; or being continually solicitous and generous to cover the urge for cruelty; or constantly assertive as a defence against unconscious wishes to be passive and dependent (Rycroft 1972). Seen in this context, the vindictive personality could be understood as a character defence against deep-seated shame, envy and feelings of vulnerability (which in turn have developed in response to difficult early experiences such as trauma). Through vindictiveness, the person obsessively tries to avenge their sense of grievance and perceived disadvantage, whilst at the same time hiding their profound sense of vulnerability and hopelessness.

The obsessive need for revenge is brilliantly portrayed in Emily Brönte's *Wuthering Heights*, the tragic tale of Heathcliff who, as a young and impoverished orphan living on the streets of Liverpool, is given a home by the warm-hearted Mr Earnshaw. Earnshaw's son, Hindley, is enraged by his father's act of kindness towards Heathcliff, and he repeatedly beats and humiliates the young orphan. Heathcliff grows up thirsting for vengeance on Hindley for having so deeply shamed him and, crucially, for having deprived him of the one person he was attached to, his beloved Cathy Earnshaw. Although over time Heathcliff eventually destroys Hindley, the satisfaction he derives from this act of revenge does not last. Still deeply aggrieved, he goes on to wreak revenge on everyone associated with Hindley, including Hindley's son Hareton whom Heathcliff raises as an uneducated servant boy. Heathcliff tries to destroy the lives of all those around him and although he succeeds in causing a great deal of suffering to many, he remains as aggrieved as ever, and dies a haunted, broken man.

(iv) Deep mistrust of others

The pressing need for revenge is often fuelled by paranoid delusions which can make the individual feel that he has been harmed when, objectively, no harm has actually been done to him. This sense of having been harmed may drive him to seek revenge but, although this revenge makes perfect sense to the individual concerned, to those around him, it is unwarranted aggression and destructiveness.

We may all have paranoid thoughts or moments of psychotic anxiety from time to time, but in a small number of people paranoid thinking dominates the mind. For some, this can be the only way to protect themselves from a terrible reality which they at one time had to endure, and which they continue to live in fear of. They are so alert to the possibility of harm that they may see it at every turn.

Paranoia can in a curious way help a person feel safe, because they take comfort from knowing that they are constantly on guard against (imagined) dangers. At the same time, being on guard in this way results in an ever-more terrifying world for the person concerned. Michael Balint, a Hungarian-born psychoanalyst who came to England in 1938, described his clinical experience with a patient whose early life was emotionally impoverished and who as an adult had become utterly convinced that everyone other than himself was malicious and menacing. Balint observed that people such as this patient often succeed in creating a world for themselves which is shaped by their most frightening fantasies (Balint 1952). Paradoxically, the paranoid individual who inhabits this sort of fearful world constantly feels that he must pre-empt the terror which has in fact already happened to him, although he may not consciously remember it happening. The need to pre-empt terror gives rise to a compelling urge for radical revenge against people who, in the perpetrator's mind, are both unconsciously bound up with the harms that were suffered in the past, and who threaten his future.

Shame, revenge and the importance of context

One of the ideas put forward in this chapter is that proportionality is an important criterion for distinguishing ordinary revenge from more radical forms. But ideas about proportionality are culturally determined. In other words, what would be considered in one context to be a proportionate response to being shamed may be regarded as wholly excessive or unreasonable in another. Take the example of suicide. In some settings, suicide represents an extreme and shocking way to punish others, as it can present those left behind with terrible feelings of guilt, regret and self-recrimination that can be difficult to work through. But suicide can have different meanings in different cultures. The anthropologist Dorothy Counts shows in a fascinating study that suicide in the Kaliai area of Papua New Guinea is a socially accepted, relatively structured, and not uncommon form of revenge for an abused wife to take against her abuser. The abused woman who decides to take revenge through suicide must follow a clearly prescribed set of rules so as to ensure that her surviving family will be entitled either to take further revenge on the man who drove her to suicide, or to receive suitable compensation from him. The rules she must follow include wearing her finest clothes when she kills herself, warning others of her intentions beforehand, and being explicit about who she feels is responsible for her death. Certain methods of suicide are accepted (drinking poison, hanging, or jumping from a tree), others are not. As Counts says, in this community (as well as a number of others), "suicide is an institutionalized and culturally recognized alternative for those who are abused, shamed and powerless, permitting them to shift the burden of humiliation from themselves to their tormentors and to enjoy some measure of vengeance against those who drove them to the act" (Counts 1987). It feels difficult to refer to any suicide as ordinary revenge, and yet that may be the case in this particular context, in so far as it is considered reasonable and proportionate, and meets the criteria of intentionality and culpability.

A more complex illustration of how understandings of proportionality are context-dependent can be found in the case of so-called honour killings. Murders that are committed in the name of a family's honour take place most commonly in parts of the Middle East and southwest Asia, but a number of communities within the US, the UK and other parts of Europe are also known to carry out these violent practices. These murders are carried out in rigidly patriarchal settings where a woman's honour is defined by her father, brothers, uncles and husbands, who feel that their own honour depends on the woman's behaviour. Where male relatives believe a female member of the family has brought dishonour onto the family, they feel justified in taking brutal revenge, even to the extent of killing her. The dishonour that women may be accused of bringing on their families is invariably linked to sex and sexuality: a woman can be put to death for having been raped, for having an extra-marital sexual relationship, or for engaging in unsupervised conversations with men who are not family members. Punishment can also be meted out if a woman requests a divorce, or refuses to go ahead with an arranged marriage. The causes vary, but in all cases the male relatives consider themselves to be the rightful arbiters of whether the woman has brought dishonour onto the family and of how the family's honour can best be restored. In thousands of cases every year, fathers, brothers, husbands, sons and uncles take violent and often murderous revenge against women whom they believe have dishonoured them.

In a damning report on honour killings, the journalist Robert Fisk describes the practice as a crime against humanity. It is difficult not to share his sense of horror when reading Fisk's account of cases such as the man who rapes his own daughter and eventually kills her, purportedly in order to save the family's honour because she has become pregnant; or the sixteen-year-old girl buried beneath a chicken coop for shaming the family by making friends with boys; or the thirteen-year-old girl who was raped and then stoned to death for what was called adultery. For those of us who regard these acts as violent expressions of hate-filled misogyny, it is difficult to think of them as anything other than irredeemably shameful and morally unacceptable[4]. Yet those who perpetrate this sort of revenge would argue that it is proportionate to the harm caused by the victims to their family's honour. What does this mean then for the use of 'proportionality' as a criterion for the ordinariness – or radicalness – of particular acts of revenge?

The position taken here is in keeping with Alison Dundes Renteln's logic in her discussion on cross-cultural approaches to validating international human rights, namely that while we recognise that the perpetrators of honour killings themselves regard their practices to be proportionate revenge, this does not require us to concur that their revenge is reasonable or proportionate. As Renteln puts it, "There is no reason why a relativist could not condemn a practice elsewhere on the basis of his own values. A relativist simply recognizes the fact that the object of criticism may be considered moral in its own system" (Dundes Renteln 1988). Similarly, many of the cases of revenge that are described in this book are regarded as radical, disproportionate and objectionable; yet at the same it seems important to acknowledge that the perpetrators themselves will have felt their acts of revenge were justified, necessary and proportionate to the harms they believed they had suffered. Understanding their actions from their points of view may in the longer term help us to address, and even prevent, some future cases of radical revenge.

**   **   **   **   **

The paradox of revenge lies in the divaricate role that shame plays: on the one hand it provokes the urge for revenge; on the other hand, the fear of being shamed is a powerful moderating force when it comes to acting on that urge. The next three chapters examine what happens when the urge for radical revenge is so compelling that the individual is able to overcome external obstacles and internal resistances, including any sense of shame about the boundless destructiveness of their actions. Chapter Two explores

---

4   The link between misogyny and radical revenge is explored in Chapter Three.

the stories of three mass shooters whose feelings of grievance, desperation and paranoia were so acute that they became inured to any sense of shame regarding their radical revenge. Chapter Three shows how people who use the internet for cruel and extreme acts of revenge sidestep feelings of shame by hiding behind online anonymity, and by splitting their online self from what they consider to be their 'real life' self. And Chapter Four looks at how a political leader's shameless promotion of vindictive policies can legitimise similar shamelessness in his followers who – feeling protected by their leader and hidden by virtue of belonging to a large group – will call for radical revenge against people who are blamed for grievances that they have not in fact caused.

Chapter Two
Mass Shootings

When mass shootings are reported in the media, the word 'senseless' comes up time and again. President Obama deplored as "senseless tragedy" the 2017 Las Vegas shooting in which 58 people were killed and more than 800 injured, and he referred to the deaths of nine people in the 2015 mass shooting at a church in North Carolina as "senseless murder". After the 2011 shooting in Tucson which killed six and injured more than 10 others (including former Congresswoman Gabrielle Giffords), President Obama told the country that "this senseless and terrible act of violence" had no place in a free society. Journalists have similarly highlighted the irrationality and futility of mass shootings, as have religious and community leaders. Their emphasis on the senselessness of mass shootings is understandable, not least because innocent people appear to be targeted at random by gunmen who seem motivated by a hate-filled rage that defies reason.

This chapter suggests that the concept of radical revenge can help to make at least some sense of these ostensibly senseless acts. The chapter focuses on three specific mass shootings and shows how in each case the shooter was so overwhelmed by feelings of grievance, shame, envy and paranoia that they were overcome by an urge for radical revenge against people who, *in the shooters' minds,* were the cause of their own pitiful states of being. The three stories described in this chapter differ in important ways, but what the three perpetrators have in common is a deep sense of shame and of grievance; a lack of clarity about the actual source of their grievances; and a compulsion to relieve themselves of their painful feelings by projecting their feelings of vulnerability and powerlessness onto people who seemed to the shooters to be in some way guilty of causing their misery.

The mass shooter

Definitions of what constitutes a mass shooting vary. While one definition is based on four or more fatalities in a single shooting incident, another requires just three deaths for a shooting incident to qualify as a mass shooting (Kelleher 1997). Some definitions are concerned with the number of injuries rather than the number of deaths and, while some include acts of terrorism, others do not. Regardless of which definition is used, the US unquestionably has one of the highest rates of mass shootings in the world, a fact that is linked at least in part to the ease of access to guns in the US.

In July 2012 a young man dressed in full riot gear and carrying four guns and 6,000 rounds of ammunition opened fire on audience members at a cinema in Aurora, Colorado. Within a short time, he had killed 12 people and injured 70 more. In the aftermath of this horrifying incident, journalists at the US magazine *Mother Jones* began an in-depth investigation into incidents which they defined as "indiscriminate rampages in public places resulting in four or more victims killed by the attacker".[5] On the basis of their research they assembled a comprehensive dataset on US mass shootings since 1982, covering a range of shooters' demographics including age, race and gender, as well as information on where each shooting occurred, how many fatalities and injuries resulted, what sort of weapons were used, and brief backgrounds to each case[6] (US Mass Shootings 1982–2018).

One of the most striking features that stand out in the *Mother Jones* database is the gender bias: 106 out of the 110 cases that are listed were perpetrated by men[7]. In terms of ethnicity, two-thirds of shooters were

5 *Mother Jones* changed their working definition of mass shooting in 2013 to three or more victims killed, in line with the new definition adopted by the federal investigation of mass shooting which was authorised that year by President Barak Obama.

6 *Mother Jones* updates the database regularly. At the time of writing, there were a total 110 cases listed.

7 Recent studies have highlighted a further, vitally important feature of mass shootings, namely the clear link between domestic violence and mass shooting. Research carried out by Bloomberg News in 2020 found that between 2014 and 2019, almost 60% of shooting incidents with at least four casualties were perpetrated by someone with a

classified as white, with the remaining third being either Black, Latino, Asian or Native American. Taken together, school shootings and workplace shootings accounted for roughly half of all cases of mass shooting and, although school shootings have received more media coverage than most other shooting incidents, nearly 30% of all mass shootings have taken place in workplaces, usually carried out by disgruntled or angry (ex)-employees (Dunbar-Ortiz 2018).

A relatively high number of cases have ended with the perpetrator dying, either by suicide or in a shoot-out with the police. Forty-two of the 110 cases reported by *Mother Jones* ended with the shooter committing suicide, and a further twenty-two were killed by police during or immediately after the shoot-out[8]. In many cases the shooter intends, or at least expects, to be killed by police during the shooting, and the term 'suicide-by-cop' has been coined to describe this manner of death (Hagan et al 2015).

As part of its continuing effort to reduce the incidence of mass shootings, the US Federal Bureau of Investigation (FBI) attempted to assemble a profile of what could be considered the typical mass shooter. In order to do this, they studied the characteristics of 63 shooters. They found that 94% were male, and a majority (63%) were white. The average age of the shooters in this study was 37 years. Apart from what they could extrapolate from these sorts of demographics, the study's authors were hard pushed to identify significant trends or patterns. They concluded that "there is no one 'profile' of an active shooter" (Silver et al 2018).

The FBI study nevertheless offers important insights. First, contrary to the popular notion that the mass shooter suddenly 'snaps' and fires on the crowd, three-quarters of the FBI's sample of shooters were found to have spent at least one week planning their shootings, and well over half of the sample spent more than a month on planning.

---

history of, or in the act of, domestic violence. The more casualties there were in an incident of mass shooting, the more likely it was that the shooter had a history of violence against women (Gu 2020).

8 In one case, the shooter tried to kill himself by swallowing insecticide but failed, and was then executed by the state of South Carolina eight years later.

Second, the study challenges the "common but erroneous inclination to assume that anyone who commits an active shooting must *de facto* be mentally ill" (Silver et al 2018, p.17). The FBI study found that while many in their sample were suffering from what were labelled as stressors (such as depression, financial pressures, conflicts with family or friends, and substance abuse) only a quarter of the sample had been diagnosed with a mental illness of any kind. (This finding probably indicates a significant degree of under-diagnosis and therefore under-treatment of mental illness rather than its low prevalence among the shooters).

Seventy-nine per cent of the FBI study sample were reported to be acting on the basis of a grievance of some kind. Interestingly, the authors suggest that "the grievance may itself not have been reasonable or even grounded in reality, but it appeared to serve as the rationale for the eventual attack, giving a sense of purpose to the shooter" (Silver et al 2018, p.22). Of the 50 shooters who had an identifiable grievance, nearly half also had a specific precipitating experience that led to the shootings. It is possible that in some cases this precipitating experience may have related to a breach in the individual's shame shield, but this can only be verified through further research into the FBI cases.

The Safe School Initiative report, published by the US Secret Service and Department of Education in 2004, reveals similar difficulty in constructing a comprehensive social profile of students who become school shooters. Focusing on 37 school shootings between 1974 and 2001, the authors found that few of the shooters had previously been assessed or diagnosed with a mental illness; some lived in one parent families, others in two parent families; some had school discipline problems, others did not; some were socially isolated, while others were popular. It is worth noting that 71% reported having felt bullied, persecuted or injured by others prior to the shooting; many had considered or attempted suicide; most "were known to have had difficulty coping with significant losses or personal failures"; and most had had no history of prior violent or criminal behaviour (US Secret Service & US Department of Education 2004).

The painful and humiliating experience of having been bullied, combined with the likely harbouring of other grievances, might suggest that the shootings were inspired by a desire for revenge, but not everyone agrees with this view. Peter Langman, an eminent US psychologist who has spent many years studying and writing about school shooters, argues that it is unlikely that school shooters want revenge for having been bullied because in practice, shooters very rarely aim their guns at the people who may in the past have harassed them. On the contrary, Langman says, some shooters, far from having been bullied, were themselves school bullies. He acknowledges that some shooters had previously experienced teasing and insults but he argues that teasing alone cannot be seen as a cause of the shooting because if it were, "there would be murders every day at every school in the nation" (Langman 2009).

Langman is not alone in this view. Writing in *The Guardian* about the mass shooting at the Marjory Stoneman Douglas High School in Parkland, Florida, Dave Cullen argues that the common image of the school shooter as a bullied outcast is based on a pernicious myth. Cullen accepts that most shooters are depressed, distressed and desperate but, like Langman, he rejects the notion that school shootings are motivated by revenge. He points out that shooters rarely aim for specific individuals, and are in fact much more concerned with achieving an "impressive body count". For Cullen, killing as many people as possible is the main aim of the school shooter who wishes above all to get widespread attention through what Cullen calls "spectacle murders" (Cullen 2019a).

Langman and Cullen are right to suggest that mass shootings cannot be explained in terms of *ordinary* revenge. They each indirectly highlight the fact that the criteria of proportionality, intentionality and culpability clearly do not apply in cases of mass shooting where, as Langman points out, the targets are often not (in any external reality sense) the individuals who have caused the shooters' grievances. However, by drawing on the concept of *radical* revenge, it becomes possible to get a different perspective on mass shootings and, in at least some cases, to make some sense of what otherwise appears to be senseless violence and destruction.

Three mass shooters

Before applying the concept of radical revenge to the three cases below, a number of important caveats need to be made.

Firstly, although the concept of 'radical revenge' helps to understand the three cases examined in this chapter, further research would be needed in order to establish whether the concept could be usefully applied to other (or all) mass shootings.

Secondly, this chapter explores mass shootings chiefly from the point of view of the three shooters so as to understand whether, and in what ways, they were (consciously or otherwise) motivated by an urge for radical revenge. By taking their point of view into consideration I am not seeking to exonerate the shooters or condone their actions, but rather to understand what led them to do what they did and, in particular, to get some idea of what their actions meant to them.

Ideally, I would have spoken with the three shooters and heard them explain in their own words how they accounted for their actions. But this was not possible. Two of the shooters died during their shoot-out, and my request for an interview with the third shooter was politely declined by his attorney who explained that it might affect ongoing legal proceedings. However, despite the impossibility of making direct contact, I felt I could get a significant glimpse into the shooters' thoughts and feelings by drawing on key primary sources. In the first case, the shooter left behind a 100,000-word memoir as well as some video testimony; in the second case, I was able to draw on a 45-page transcript of the shooter's police interview which had taken place just hours after the shooting; and in the third case I could give some thought to the shooter's suicide note.

The availability of these materials was a significant factor in choosing to focus on these three particular perpetrators. As it happens, the three shooters also fit in with a number of the characteristics highlighted in the *Mother Jones* database: they are all male; two of them are white, the third was Eurasian; two died during the shooting and one survived; one was a school shooter, one a workplace shooter, and one was neither; and they all had easy access to the guns they used.

The third caveat to be made is that although I draw on psychoanalytic concepts to describe certain aspects of these cases, I am neither attempting, nor claiming in any way, to have some sort of privileged access to the psyches of the individuals that I am writing about. I can only speculate on their inner worlds and surmise what their grievances may have been on the basis of what they have said or written, supplemented by information from police reports, media accounts and other sources. Warning against the perils of wild analysis, Freud wisely reminds us that psychoanalysis "absolutely requires a fairly long period of contact with the patient" (Freud 1910).

(i) Elliot Rodger

Elliot Rodger was 22 years old when he stabbed to death his two flatmates and their friend before driving to a nearby college campus in Alta Vista, California where he planned to shoot and kill as many members of the Alpha Phi sorority house as possible. In the event, he killed two members of the sorority and injured a third before driving off. From his car window he saw a group of young people and, as they moved from the pavement into a shop, he shot at them and killed one of the young men. Still driving, Elliot shot at a number of pedestrians, and rammed his car into others. Minutes later he crashed the car and shot himself in the head. In addition to killing himself, Elliot Rodger had killed six people and injured 14 more.

Between committing the stabbings and the shootings, Elliot took the time to upload a video on YouTube, in which he made it clear that he regarded the killings as "revenge against humanity". Full of emotion, he says:

> ...ever since I hit puberty, I've been forced to endure an existence of loneliness, rejection and unfulfilled desires all because girls have never been attracted to me. ...I don't know why you girls aren't attracted to me, but I will punish you all for it. It's an injustice, a crime because... I don't know what you don't see in me. I'm the perfect guy and yet you throw yourselves at all these obnoxious men instead of me, the supreme gentleman. I will

punish all of you for it. (Langman 2014, transcript of Rodger's Retribution video)

In addition to his rage at all the girls whom he felt had rejected him, Elliot went on to berate his rivals, namely all the men who, he believed,

> looked down upon me every time I tried to go out and join them, they've *all* treated me like a mouse. Well now I will be a god compared to you. You will *all* be animals. You are animals and I will slaughter you like animals. (*my italics*)

The reason for emphasising the word *all* is to highlight the fact that by the time of the shootings, Elliot's paranoid ideation was such that every young woman he encountered not only represented those who had in the past rejected him: in his mind they *were* those women. As far as Elliot was concerned, they were all guilty of shaming and hurting him and they deserved to be punished. Similarly, all the young men he came across *were* the ones who had made him feel as small as a mouse, and in Elliot's mind they too deserved to be 'slaughtered' in revenge.

Along with his YouTube retribution videos, Elliot left behind a 100,000+ word dossier entitled *The Twisted World of Elliot Rodger*. In this memoir he describes his short life in granular detail, telling the reader about his feelings towards various family members and acquaintances, recounting the divorce of his parents and the subsequent changes in the family's domestic arrangements, the many children whom he met over the years, which ones had played with him and which had snubbed and shamed him, and how he had celebrated each of his birthdays. The detail with which he describes each year of his life, year by year, is remarkable and suggests a narcissistic fantasy that the minutiae of his life will be of interest to many others (Rodger, undated).

What comes through more than anything in this memoir is Elliot's profound sense of shame, and his bitter envy of others who all seemed to have what he yearned for. He describes himself in grandiose terms: born to an idealised white British father who "hailed from a prestigious and once-wealthy family" and who "impregnated" the woman who was to become Elliot's mother, a Malaysian woman of Chinese descent who had worked as a nurse. Although he later suggests some appreciation for his mother – in particular her unfailing efforts to please him by conceding to many of his demands over the years – Elliot struggled with his mixed-race background and his physical attributes. At the age of nine he realised that he felt different to what he called the "normal fully-white kids" whom he tried unsuccessfully to fit in with. He writes about how he "always envied and admired blonde-haired people", so much so that as a young boy he convinced his parents to allow him to dye his hair blonde.

Along with the colour of his hair and skin, Elliot was troubled by his relatively small physique. These were all features which distinguished him from his father whom he regarded as strong, noble and successful. Unable to identify physically with his father, Elliot began to feel ashamed of his physical self, and a rising envy for all those who, like his father, had 'made the grade'. One way to think of this is that while on the one hand Elliot idealised his father, on the other hand he was filled with an oedipal, murderous envy of him. It is likely that his inability to work through and resolve these feelings contributed to his pervasive sense of grievance and his proclivity for retribution.

The first time he could remember feeling so acutely aware of his shame and envy was at the age of six, when he was barred from an amusement park ride because of his size and was forced to watch all the other boys his age enjoying the ride. He writes that "this injustice was very small indeed compared to all the things I'll be denied in the future because of my height." Throughout his memoir, he writes of the humiliation he experienced by virtue of being relatively small. At nine he saw that he was the shortest child in the class, including the girls, which "instilled the first feelings of inferiority in me, and such feelings would only grow more volatile with time".

Although Elliot was born into a well-off middle class family, the family's wealth was significantly diminished following his parents' divorce and his father's professional setbacks. When his father had to reduce his contributions towards child maintenance, Elliot's mother was forced to move to more modest accommodation in "a lower-class area" which deepened Elliot's sense of grievance and shame.

As Elliot saw the world, he was singularly disadvantaged and he felt a burning envy towards those around him. Whereas his mother's pregnancy with him had been "unwanted", his sister who was born five years later was a "planned" baby. There is a sense of great injustice as Elliot describes how his sister was given the bedroom he had so badly wanted when the family moved house; and later, when Elliot was 12 years old and his step-mother had a baby, there was a similar resentment at having to give up his room for the new baby so that the baby could be close to the parents. Somewhat poignantly, Elliot tells his reader that part of the reason he didn't want the other room was because he was afraid of the dark. One can only speculate about the sorts of monsters that lurked in Elliot's darkness.

By his own account, puberty led to an intensification of Elliot's feelings of shame and envy. At this stage he became more acutely conscious of his envy for his father, whom he came to see as the sort of man who could attract women with ease. Elliot's envy, and the oedipal wound from which it sprang, were continuously exacerbated by seeing more and more friends and strangers living up to the ideal that his father represented, while Elliot himself remained unable to do so. Even his much younger half-brother, who was tall for his age and who was able to make friends with ease, put him to shame. Elliot writes that eventually he came to the conclusion that he would have to kill his half-brother in retribution, despite having fond feelings for him because the little boy looked up to him.

By the time he was 16 years old, Elliot felt there was nothing he could do to reverse what he felt was the unfairness of his life. He writes that at this stage he felt completely powerless, and his only way of dealing with these painful feelings was by escaping into the world of online games, including the computer game *World of Warcraft*, which at one point, he says, he became addicted to.

Although video games were important, Elliot's memoir indicates that there was another, more structured way that Elliot managed his feelings of shame, envy and powerlessness. This was through narcissistic defences that involved the relentless denigration of the people whom he regarded as foes and rivals. Through this, he could deny the feelings of shame that arose from his inability to talk with a girl, let alone kiss or have any sort of sexual relations with her. Increasingly, he defended himself against his humiliation and anxiety by disparaging the boys whom he envied (like his father) for their 'success' with these hateful – but deeply desired – girls. He is particularly scathing when writing about non-white boys, asking "How could an inferior, ugly black boy be able to get a white girl and not me? I am beautiful, and I am half white myself. I am descended from British aristocracy. He is descended from slaves. I deserve it more." When his new (white) roommate tells Elliot about an ex-girlfriend, Elliot again defends narcissistically against his deflated feelings:

> I didn't understand how a chubby and unattractive guy like Spencer would have been able to get a girlfriend, while I've never had a chance to...I concluded to myself that this former 'girlfriend' of his that he mentioned must have been just as unattractive as he was. There was no need for me to be jealous. (Rodger, undated)

Elliot describes a number of attempts to make new friends, to feel accepted by the cool kids and ultimately to find a girl willing to be his girlfriend. These efforts were unsuccessful, and his feelings of failure and shame were repeatedly projected onto others, including the boys whom he envied with rage, or the blonde-haired girls whom he desired and despised in equal measure. He was dismissive of all those who tried to help him, including the various counsellors and psychiatrists he was sent to and the family friends who tried to advise him on how to make friends. These benign figures in his life were regarded by Elliot at best as misguided and at worst as part of the problem, namely successful people who were only helping him in order to "boost...their already big egos".

Having long attributed his failures to being of mixed race, Elliot eventually encountered a piece of reality which made this belief difficult to maintain. He describes the experience which took place while he was at a party.

I came across this Asian guy who was talking to a white girl. The sight of that filled me with rage. I always felt as if white girls thought less of me because I was half-Asian, but then I see this white girl at the party talking to a full-blooded Asian. I never had that kind of attention from a white girl! ... How could an ugly Asian attract the attention of a white girl, while a beautiful Eurasian like myself never had any attention from them? I thought with rage. (Rodger, undated)

Emboldened by alcohol, Elliot approached the couple which had so enraged him, and he physically bumped the Asian boy aside. However, in his drunken state, Elliot himself then fell to the ground, thereby suffering further humiliation.

This incident was the beginning of what became the final breach to Elliot's shame shield. Still under the influence of alcohol, he got back up on his feet and while doing so he saw a group of boys and girls sitting on a ledge, happily chatting and laughing. He felt outraged that the girls failed to pay any attention to him. When he insulted them, the boys and girls simply laughed at him and returned the insults. This, he says, "was the last straw. I had taken enough insults that night. A dark, hate-fuelled rage overcame my entire being and I tried to push as many of them as I could from the 10-foot ledge". In the event, he was the one to fall from the ledge in a most humiliating turn of events. As he got back up he realised his treasured Gucci sunglasses were missing. Assuming they had somehow been stolen from him, he returned to the party to retrieve them. Before long, he encountered the people that he had been pushing around. They greeted him with mockery and insults. Shamed and powerless, he was then beaten up. He writes: "I had never been beaten and humiliated that badly. Everyone in Isla Vista saw what happened, and it was truly horrific."

He writes with deep self-pity and diminishing insight that, although he was suffering a broken leg, no girl had offered to help him return to his room, nor did they offer to sleep with him to make him feel better. He felt completely unloved, uncared for and alone. It seems that this was the turning point, the final violation to Elliot's fragile sense of self. He writes:

The highly unjust experience of being beaten and humiliated in front of everyone at Isla Vista, and their subsequent lack of concern for my well-being, was the last and final straw. I actually gave them all one last chance to accept me, to give me a reason not to hate them, and they devastatingly blew it back in my face. I gave the world too many chances. It was time for Retribution.

At this point, Elliot began plotting his revenge, evidently taking solace and indeed pleasure from the act of planning his ultimate act of retribution. He hastily, and evidently without much difficulty, purchased a semi-automatic pistol from a local gun shop. He describes the new feeling of power and manliness he experienced just by holding the weapon in his hand. After saving up money from the allowance and gifts he received from his parents and grandmothers he bought a second gun, and then later a third one which he intended to use for his suicide immediately following the shootings that he intended to carry out.

As he approaches the end of his memoir, having described his plan to wreak revenge on all those who had rejected and shamed him, Elliot's narcissism takes a floridly psychotic turn:

Humanity has never accepted me among them, and now I know why. I am more than human. I am superior to them all. I am Elliot Rodger...Magnificent, glorious, supreme, eminent. Divine! I am the closest thing there is to a living god. Humanity is a disgusting, depraved, and evil species. It is my purpose to punish them all...I will truly be a powerful god, punishing everyone I deem to be impure and depraved. (Rodger, undated)

This self-aggrandisement appears to corroborate Dave Cullen's idea that mass shooters are simply 'spectacle murderers' who are motivated by a desire for fame or infamy. However, at best this explains only part of what was going on for Elliot. Given all that he wrote about himself, it seems that he was 'performing' not only to impress (or horrify) an external audience but, more importantly, he was trying to rid himself of the shame he felt under the gaze of his own mind's eye. Elliot needed to feel that he had met the demands of his ego ideal: that he was a strong and masculine man like his father, and that he was able to take what he believed were strong and masculine measures in order to assert his sense of self.

After the stabbings, shootings and his suicide in 2014, Elliot Rodger became something of a hero to a newly formed group which met online. The group, known as incels (which stands for 'involuntary celibates'), is made up of boys and men who bitterly resent the fact that they have never had sexual relations with a woman, something which they believe they are entitled to simply by virtue of being male. Incels hold all women responsible for this perceived injustice, as well as all the men whom women choose in preference to the incels. Yet what Elliot's memoir makes clear is that his murderous violence was not simply revenge for not having had sex. To paraphrase Peter Langman, simply not having had the sexual experiences that one desires cannot be said to cause mass murder: if it did, there would be many, many more murders in the world! Elliot was taking revenge for all the shame and humiliation he had experienced throughout his life, and from which his fragile sense of self had never recovered. Consciously, he had focussed on the rejections he suffered from the cool boys and blond girls, but, as his memoir indicates, there were many other deep-rooted sources of shame and many other narcissistic wounds which eventually brought Elliot to the utter hopelessness that had overwhelmed him by the time he carried out his brutal killings.

The retribution that Elliot planned and detailed in his memoir was an act of radical revenge: not only in its destructiveness and lack of proportionality, but also because it did not meet the criteria of culpability or intentionality. Elliot's victims had the tragic misfortune of looking similar to, or being otherwise associated with, those whom he felt had maligned or deprived him. The fact that these victims were *representative* of something very painful had become lost on Elliot. By the time of the killings, as far as Elliot was concerned, these people (and indeed *all* people) *actually were* the cause of his bitterness and resentment. His paranoid ideation, the psychotic belief that all of these people – in fact all people – had rejected him, brought him to the point where killing others, and himself, felt like the only way to assert his delusional sense of self, and rid himself of unbearable feelings of despair and powerlessness. His narcissistic and increasingly psychotic defences, which he clung to right until the end, had ultimately failed him.

(ii) Jesse Osborne

In November 2019, Jesse Osborne was sentenced to life in prison without parole for fatally shooting his father and a six-year-old boy at a nearby elementary school, and for attempting to murder two other children and a teacher at the same school. Jesse had just turned 14 years old when he committed these crimes in the small rural community of Townville, South Carolina.

According to newspaper and television reports, Jesse was a cold-blooded, gun-obsessed killer who had boasted online that he was going to kill 50 or 60 people, and who had shown no remorse after the shootings. It is difficult to square this chilling description of the 14-year-old with the image of Jesse Osborne that emerges from his interview with two law enforcement officers just hours after the shootings. Jesse did not have a parent or lawyer present during the interview with the two officers, one of whom was a male police investigator from the local County Sheriff's Office and the other a female FBI agent; nor did he think to ask for a lawyer or parent to accompany him. He seems to have been so unguarded and guileless in what he told the officers that it is not clear whether he fully understood the purpose of the police interview, or what the implications would be for subsequent court proceedings. From the transcript of the interview it appears that Jesse was in shock after committing the shootings. His guilelessness may also have had something to do with the manner in which the officers spoke with him. They offered him food and drink from McDonald's, acknowledged that he had had a "very rough day", and they listened to him with patience and apparent concern while gently prompting him to answer their questions. Jesse may have been relieved to have had an opportunity to talk about what had happened, to verbalise some of the confusion that was going on in his mind, and to tell someone – anyone – something of what he had been going through. He seems to have been naïvely unaware that the main purpose of the interview was to gain evidence for the prosecution. At the end of the meeting, he thanked the officers for talking with him and told them it was nice meeting them.

My interpretation of the Townville mass shooting is based almost entirely on the transcript of this police interview (State of South Carolina 2016). As a result, my account will be limited and largely one-sided, but by focussing on Jesse's own version of events I am in a better position to understand at least some of what was going on for him before and during his act of radical revenge.

Jesse Osborne grew up a rather isolated, lonely and troubled boy. He went to a local school up to eighth grade, but at the age of 13 he switched to home schooling. He said he had been bullied at every school he had attended, and by the time he was in sixth grade the bullying had turned physical, including being "ganged up" against by groups of classmates every time he went to use the toilet. Eventually, unable to bear the shame and fear of being bullied, Jesse brought a hatchet and machete into school. He kept the weapons hidden in a bag (perhaps just knowing that he had the weapons was enough to make himself feel secretly powerful) but before long they were discovered by the school authorities. Jesse was arrested, sentenced to a spell in a juvenile detention facility, and then expelled from school. After this, he was "home schooled", a lonely experience consisting of online lessons without regular personal contact with teachers or fellow-students.

Jesse lived at home in Townville with his mother and father. His siblings were quite a bit older and had moved away from home. Jesse told the officers who interviewed him that he had recently been "isolating himself" at home so that his father would not be able to "fuss" at him. When his father (who many years previously had been arrested for domestic violence) did "fuss", Jesse would take himself downstairs, but then, he said, his mother would get fussed at, at which point Jesse would go back up and tell both parents to stop fussing. The night before the shootings, Jesse's father

> was fussing to me and my mom about not getting paid enough for
> his chicken houses. And he was getting up in my face and stuff.

And whenever he's drunk, he always like says he wants to fight me because I make this face to him. And he'll — and then my mom will have to step in and get fussed at too. And last night he was just worse than he's ever been. He was just drinking. (State of South Carolina 2016)

It is unfortunate (but not altogether surprising) that the officers did not at any time ask Jesse what exactly he meant by "fussing". This could have been helpful for understanding what the circumstances were that ultimately provoked Jesse to take his extreme measures. We are left to speculate whether fussing was simply nagging, or whether it was a euphemism for something altogether more sinister. It seems likely it was the latter, given the testimony that was later presented in court by Jesse's half-brother who spoke under oath about the occasions when Jesse's father would make Jesse pull down his trousers and would beat him with sticks or a belt until the boy's screaming could be heard throughout the house. Moreover, Jesse's paternal grandfather testified that his son (Jesse's father) had threatened him with violence so that he felt he had to carry a gun for protection whenever they met. Whatever the "fussing" consisted of, it had clearly been going on for some time, and had been increasingly difficult for Jesse to bear, both on his own behalf and his mother's. Jesse's description of his father 'getting in his face' on the night before the shootings evokes a feeling of stifling menace. The next day, Jesse said, his father began fussing again and "I was like, this is it. I ran...and then went in and shot him three times. And then I freaked out."

For many years Jesse had lived with feelings of helplessness, rejection and vulnerability. At school he had been shamed by fellow students who bullied and excluded him. At home he was unable to protect himself, or his mother, from his father's continued provocations. Unable to bear any more fussing, and feeling powerless to stop it in any other way, Jesse shot his father. However, rather than providing Jesse with relief, shooting his father caused him to panic; in Jesse's words, it 'freaked him out'. What immediately followed the shooting seems to have been an overwhelming feeling of confusion, dissociation and a defensive break from external reality.

Jesse's description of events suggests a deep split in his ego. Alongside the enraged and vengeful adolescent who shot his father in the back three times there is a bewildered little boy who told the police officers that Floppy, his pet rabbit, was his best friend. He described how, straight after shooting his father, he ran upstairs to give Floppy and his pet dogs a goodbye kiss. At one point while talking with the police he spoke of the wounded "little baby rabbit" he once found. "I got it and put it in a box and nurtured it for a couple of days," he said. "It finally died from not having its mama". (It may be that he himself was unconsciously feeling wounded and wishing for maternal nurturing and protection.) The little-boy-Jesse explains to the officers that he loves animals, "because they can't hurt — well, they can't emotionally hurt you." This is the Jesse who speaks with love and longing for his grandparents, his Papa and Nanna, whom he phoned as soon as his gun had jammed during the school shooting to tell them "what happened". (The passive verb here suggests a dissociated sense of terrible things having somehow happened, rather than he himself having made these things happen.) He tells the police officers that he really hopes his mom and grandparents are okay, and that they don't have a heart attack, because they had said to him (presumably when he had been sent to the juvenile detention centre) that if he ever went back to jail they'd have a heart attack.

The split in Jesse's ego was bewildering for him. He could see, but also could not see, that the children whom he went on to shoot after having killed his father were not the children who had at one time bullied him. After shooting his father and kissing his pet animals goodbye, Jesse had taken his guns and driven three miles to the elementary school that he had once attended, and opened fire on the playground. According to one report, Jesse screamed "I hate my life" as he pulled the trigger. When the interviewing officer asked Jesse if the kids at his school were a little rough, he replied yes but, importantly, he added that "it wasn't those kids there. It was just the past kids before that". The officer asks, "So you didn't really have personal animosity against anyone at the school?" to which Jesse replies, "I just had a problem with the school." Later in the police interview, Jesse says with even greater clarity, "the kids did nothing to me".

The split in Jesse's ego becomes evident in his ambivalence between wanting to die, and wanting to live; and between wanting to kill the school children, and thinking, in the moment of the shooting, "what am I doing?". This sense of dissociation continues through during the interview, as in the following exchange about the killing of his father:

Jesse: I just seen him slump over. I thought I missed the first time, so I shot him two more. Then I seen him slump over, and I was like, 'what have I just did? [sic] I can't go back now.' So— It's already done. But I'm pretty sure he's dead. I'm hoping he's not, but I'm pretty sure he is.

Officer: Well, what was your ultimate goal? I mean, what— you know, if you know you shot your dad and you knew you went over to the school and some kids got hurt there, what were you looking— I mean, were you planning to take your own life?

Jesse: Yeah. Because I was just done. I was just done. Bullying by all these people. And I was like, 'okay, I can't take all this hatred anymore'. So I was like, 'Yeah, I might as well kill myself before I go to jail.' But I'm glad I didn't because now I have a life. Probably won't get a job, but I'll – I'll at least have a life. (State of South Carolina 2016)

Jesse's expectation that he may "at least have a life" extended to hoping that he would end up in a juvenile detention centre where "there's an actual school there", because he wanted to be able to study history which, he explained, is his favourite subject. Childlike, he seems to have had no understanding of the external reality of his situation, which included the possibility (which later became a reality) that he would be put on trial as an adult rather than a juvenile and, ultimately, be sentenced to life in prison. (Jesse evaded the death penalty because ten years previously the US Supreme Court had ruled that it is unconstitutional to sentence someone to death if they were under 18 years of age at the time of their crime.)

Jesse's isolation, desperation and anger do not entirely explain his actions. Two other factors emerge from the interview. The first concerns the easy availability of guns and Jesse's familiarity with using them. He explains that his father kept a number of guns in their home. Guns appear to have had an important function in Jesse's family life, and at one point he says that shooting "relieves my stress". The officer asks if Jesse's family have a little shooting range in their yard, and Jesse answers that "we shoot at, like, a water heater and washer and there's hundreds of bullet holes in those". This normalisation of lethal weapons in Jesse's family life will almost certainly have made it easier for him, in his desperation, to take the gun from his father's nightstand drawer, fill it with "cheap ammo", and use it to kill his victims[9].

The second crucial contextual factor was the online 'community' that Jesse had become involved with. Jesse was a young adolescent boy apparently without friends, who had been bullied, isolated and rejected. It comes as no surprise that he found solace in online communities; as he said, "I finally found people to actually talk to me". The 'community' was a group of people who claimed to be angry with their schools too. Jesse was convinced that "they were my friends and stuff, and they said they were all going to shoot up their schools too". He described his Instagram chats with what he calls the "true crime community", but warns the police officer not to engage with this group, because it is "basically people obsessed with mass murderers and serial killers". But these were, he believed, his only friends, so when they encouraged him to plan a school shooting – when, as he said, they began "cheering me on" – Jesse rose to the bait. It was in this context that Jesse began boasting in the days and weeks before the shooting that he planned to kill 50 or 60 people. He was trying to get the approval and admiration of these faceless internet 'friends' who were egging him on to make bombs and to 'kill the scumbags'. One of the police officers drew attention to the mix of confusion and fantasy in Jesse's mind when he asked, "How were you

---

9   It was this cheap ammo which eventually jammed the gun, which in turn prevented Jesse from killing more people.

going to kill that many kids with one gun?". Jesse replied, "Honestly, I don't know"[10].

(iii) Mark Barton

On 29 July 1999, 44-year-old Mark Barton armed himself with a .9mm Glock semi-automatic hand gun and a .45 Colt semi-automatic pistol. Secure in the knowledge that he had another two guns and 200 rounds of ammunition stored in his van, Barton walked into the Atlanta, Georgia day trading company where he had once worked. Declaring that "it's been a bad trading day and it's about to get worse", he began shooting whoever he saw. Within a short time, he had killed nine people and injured a further 13 in two separate workplaces. As police cars began to arrive, he ran back to his van and drove away, with the police not far behind him. When he realised he was cornered, Barton used one of his guns to kill himself. A suicide note was later found along with the bodies of his wife, 11-year-old son and eight-year-old daughter whom he had murdered in the days before the shooting spree.

Most accounts attribute Mark Barton's acts of violence to the heavy financial debts he had accumulated through online day trading in shares. Although these debts undoubtedly played a key role in his unravelling, a closer look at what was going on for Barton reveals a much darker picture which goes back to his earlier life. We know something of Mark Barton's background from the flurry of media reports which followed the shootings, and from a book written a few years later by his erstwhile colleague, Brent

---

10 The *Encyclopedia Dramatica* – a nasty website dedicated to deriding individuals – gives a flavour of the sort of online community that Jesse Osborne had become involved with. This website has a page devoted to Jesse's crimes, describing him as an "Americunt" who failed in his mission, although "frankly, no one gave a fuck about his chimpout". Jesse is given a score of 40 out of 100 for his shootings, and is compared unfavourably with other mass shooters. The site concludes: "All he has left to enjoy is getting his scrawny ass buttfucked during Bubba's daily routine". The people whom Jesse mistook as his friends were in fact odious and rather pitiful, preying on a 14-year-old loner who evidently was unable to distinguish between genuine friendship on the one hand, and manipulation and malice on the other.

Doonan (whom Barton shot twice at close range) (Doonan 2006). And there is Barton's suicide note, too. Taken together, these sources suggest that while Barton's financial losses were serious, it was a more deep-rooted envy, anger and paranoia, together with a terrible sense of shame and grievance, that brought him to his violent end.

Mark Barton grew up with his father who served in the US Air Force, and mother who worked as a secretary at a local Methodist church. An only child, he spent most of his early years in Sumter, South Carolina. By all accounts he was a gifted student who excelled in chemistry, but was not popular with his peers. He seems to have been something of a loner at school, almost to the point of having been invisible. According to one account, his name was listed incorrectly in his yearbook two years in a row (he was called 'Jack Barton' in 1971, and 'Mack Barton' in 1972) and on a third occasion, the yearbook did not include his photo at all. It is reasonable to assume that this reflected his peers' lack of regard or interest in him, which would probably have shamed and hurt the rather isolated high school student. Journalists who researched Barton's background found that some of his fellow-students did not remember him, while others described him as not having many friends. As he got older, Barton became involved with heavy drug use and suffered a number of overdoses in late adolescence.

Different accounts emphasise different aspects of Mark Barton's life, but almost all of them highlight his acute sensitivity to insult and injury, and his readiness to respond with extreme measures. Early in his career, he was fired from his job as the general manager of a small manufacturing company because his co-workers complained of his paranoia, his stubborn grudges against colleagues, and his uncontrolled outbursts of anger when he was unable to solve work-related problems (Doonan 2006; Gegax 1999). A week after being fired, he took revenge. He broke into the company offices in the middle of the night and, after stealing data from the company's computers, he wiped the hard drives clean. He made sure to take all hard copies of the data too, so as to ensure that his revenge had the maximum destructive impact on those who had shamed him.

Barton's first marriage ended when his wife and mother-in-law were found hacked to death by a heavy instrument. Barton was the key suspect, but charges were not pressed. He is reported to have taken life insurance out on his wife a few days before her death and to have used a large portion of the sizeable pay-out from the insurance company to start afresh with the woman who was to become his second wife and his two children from the first marriage (Sack 1999). Before long, his new relationship began to suffer because of Barton's erratic and controlling behaviour, and soon there were arguments over money. Unable to take it any longer, Barton's second wife separated from him and moved out of the family home into a small apartment.

Barton had hoped to be able to make a great deal of money through trading shares, but he made a string of losses instead. Shortly after his wife moved out of their home, he was told by the day trading company All-Tech that he would no longer be allowed to trade from their premises because of his unpaid debts. Facing financial ruin and unable to keep up with his rent, Barton felt he had no option but to ask his now estranged wife to allow him and his two children to move in with her in her small apartment. To her great cost, she relented.

Barton tried one last time to turn around his financial misfortune. He took his remaining money to a company called Momentum Securities where he quickly lost it through share trading. Desperate, he borrowed a further $100,000 from Momentum Securities, but accrued further losses which made it impossible for him to pay back his loan. As a result, Momentum Securities cancelled his account.

Mark Barton could not bear any further losses, nor presumably the shame associated with his failed attempts to restore his financial standing. In addition to his financial ruin he had suffered the ignominy of having had to beg his wife to take him in; being asked to leave by All-Tech; and having his Momentum account cancelled. This last experience of having his account cancelled may have been the ultimate breach in Mark Barton's shame shield. His feelings of humiliation and his many grievances, perhaps going as far back as high school or earlier, were too much to bear. As he wrote in his suicide note, "I have come to hate this life and this system of things". It was time to take revenge against all those whom he felt had put him through this terrible pain.

Radical Revenge

Barton's first act of revenge was the murder of his second wife. He beat her with a hammer and then put her face-down in a bath tub to make sure that she was dead. In his suicide note he explains that "she was one of the main reasons for my demise". One can only speculate what Barton had in mind when he wrote this, and what exactly he blamed her for. The fact that he had ended up depending on her kindness and her financial support was a reality that was ultimately too shameful for him to bear. He had experienced an earlier narcissistic blow when she had attempted to separate from him, leaving him feeling unwanted and unloved, just as so many other people had done – at school, in his workplaces and perhaps in other, earlier parts of his life. That he then had to beg her for shelter because he could no longer afford his own housing would have compounded his feelings of failure and shame. Barton punished his wife not for his *financial* demise, but for the crashing in of his misogynistic delusion that he was the powerful one, and that she was his weak and subordinate wife.

Mark Barton explains in his suicide letter that after killing his wife, he had also killed his son and daughter. Like his wife, he "hit them with the hammer in their sleep and then put them face-down in the bathtub to make sure they did not wake up in pain." It is difficult to speculate why Barton killed his children. He himself seems unclear about this. In his letter he asks "Why did I?" and then writes, "I've been dying since October. Wake up at night so afraid, so terrified that I couldn't be that afraid while awake. It has taken its toll." It is not clear what the awful terror is that haunted him, but Barton evidently felt that whatever it was, it had been transmitted from his father to him, and that he would – or already had – transmitted it to his son. He writes: "The fears of the father are transferred to the son. It was from my father to me and from me to my son. He already had it… I had to take him with me." No indication is given as to why he killed his daughter.

Barton's paranoia, shame and terror seem to have become unbearable, and through his violence, and ultimately his suicide, he hoped to project these feelings onto those whom he blamed for his pain. "I don't plan to live very much longer," he wrote. "Just long enough to kill as many of the people that greedily sought my destruction." In Mark Barton's eyes, the killing of his wife, and the subsequent shootings at Momentum Securities and All-Tech were acts of revenge. Some of the people he shot were unknown to him, others were former colleagues. He owed money to some of them, but not to others. His revenge was 'radical', not only because of the lack of proportionality in its extreme destructiveness, but also because it had nothing to do with intentionality or culpability. Barton's own sense of failure and the accompanying feelings of shame and paranoia, and his grievance against all those who refused to collude with his delusional endeavours, all contributed to his final violent actions.

Mass shootings and radical revenge

Most observers regard mass shootings as random and senseless acts of violence. Few if any of the victims have caused harm to the shooter. In most cases they have never even met him prior to the shooting. Despite this, these people become the target of the shooter's destructive rage. What the three cases discussed in this chapter suggest is that an explosive mix of grievance, shame, rage and paranoia fill the shooter's mind such that at the time of the shooting the victims no longer *represent* the people who have made the shooter's life so painful and difficult to bear; they *are* the people to blame for his suffering. And so, filled with rage, despair and grievance, and overcome by delusion, the shooter is driven to take revenge without any reality-based thoughts of proportionality, intention, or culpability.

One question that arises is why these desperate and aggrieved individuals would choose to take their revenge so publicly. Dave Cullen has described mass shootings as spectacle murders, a phenomenon that he regards as being essentially a "performance without a cause" (Cullen 2019b). He goes further, suggesting that spectacle murder "is all about TV", implying that mass shootings are carried out by people who are desperate to have their proverbial ten minutes of fame. The three cases discussed in this chapter suggest that there is more to it than a shallow desire for fame (or notoriety). Elliot Rodger, Jesse Osborne and Mark Barton suffered profound humiliation, loneliness and vulnerability for much of their lives. By enacting their revenge in a public place, they were able to project their unbearable feelings of vulnerability not only on to those whom they shot, but on all the people present at the scene of the shooting who were thrown into a terrible panic. The shooters may have briefly felt extremely powerful and even invincible but, as the horrible reality of their lives returned to them, so too their feelings of powerlessness and hopelessness will have returned. This may help to explain why Elliott Rodger and Mark Barton (and many other mass shooters) ended up killing themselves in the aftermath of the shootings.

Conversely, Jesse Osborne did not commit suicide nor did this seem to have been part of his plan. Whereas Elliot Rodger and Mark Barton may have been thin-skinned narcissists who were easily shamed and enraged by their tormentors, Jesse was a confused and vulnerable adolescent who had been frightened and shamed by bullies both at school and at home. Isolated and desperate, he allowed himself to be cajoled into the killings by his online so-called friends. He harboured delusional thoughts that the shootings would avenge all the bullying he had been subjected to, and would transform his life by bringing him an elevated status among his new group of friends. It is significant that Jesse had a loving relationship with his grandparents and his mother, a factor which may have contributed to his ability to want to go on living after taking revenge on what he believed were his tormentors.

All three of the shooters had felt threatened and humiliated beyond endurance, and had slowly withdrawn into a lonely and isolated world in which they began to plan their revenge against those whom they blamed for their misery. This withdrawal was a defence against further shame and pain but because of the shooters' internal conflicts and their external circumstances, it was a defence that took on a dark and sinister hue. As the psychoanalyst Christopher Bollas puts it, where an individual gets caught up in a deeply paranoid state of mind, he may over time "turn inwards and become a recluse, continuously imbibing poisonous thoughts from a dark breast, and celebrating isolation as an end in itself. Tragically this internal poison can be projected outwards with extreme violence" (Bollas 2018). This paranoid state of mind was in evidence in all three cases. It led Elliot Rodger to feel cruelly humiliated by *all* cool boys and blond girls; Mark Barton felt scorned and disrespected by all those whom he associated with his failures; and in the heat of a confused moment, Jesse saw all school children as somehow implicated in his earlier experiences of being bullied at school. To the outside observer, these three shooters were guilty of killing and injuring innocent people in a random act of monstrous violence. For the shooters themselves, their actions were the only means available to escape unendurable feelings of shame, isolation and pain.

There were also significant *external* factors that led these three mass shooters to arm themselves with guns and assault weapons in order to wreak violent revenge for what they felt were intolerable grievances. One of these factors relates to the pervasive cultural associations between on the one hand being a strong and virile man and, on the other hand being willing and able to take extreme measures to punish aggressors. Film, literature and video games are replete with stories of powerful, vengeful men who go to extreme lengths to pay back their enemies and opponents. Vengeful women are often presented as crazed or catty, but men who take radical revenge are frequently portrayed as fearless heroes.

Another crucial external factor that helps to explain the prevalence and nature of mass shootings in the US is to do with the lack of gun control. In the US, guns are both lionised as the weapon of the strong, and easily available. In the three case studies, none of the shooters had any difficulty procuring their weapons. Even 14-year-old Jesse Osborne had access to a range of guns and bullets, and evidently had no qualms about pulling the trigger of these deadly weapons.

In a recent article, the British journalist Alex Hannaford reported on his study of mass shooters which he conducted in the wake of the horrific shootings at the Marjory Stoneman Douglas High School in Parkland, Florida, and at Sandy Hook Elementary School in Connecticut (Hannaford 2018). Hannaford wrote letters to roughly 50 mass shooters who were serving long-term prison sentences across the US, or who were on death row. In his letter he asked what they thought might have stopped them from doing what they did. Although the response rate was low (just under 25%), the replies which Hannaford received were illuminating. One shooter who was serving a life sentence without parole for shooting five co-workers said that if guns were not available to people with mental health problems, mass shootings would be much less common. Another respondent, who had killed his former teacher and three students with a 12-gauge pump-action shotgun and sawn-off rifle, attributed mass shootings to underlying problems such as depression, anger, and family problems, but said he hoped that guns would be outlawed to the general public one day. A third respondent, Paul Devoe, wrote to Hannaford from death row. Enraged when his landlady had asked him to move out of his home, he had gone on a 'killing spree' that resulted in six deaths. He remembers wanting to kill, but said that if he had not had a gun, it would not have happened.

One of the most moving stories was William Hardesty's. Hardesty agreed to speak with Hannaford on the phone from prison. When they spoke, Hardesty explained that he had killed seven people, including his mother and father, while he was high on drugs and alcohol. He shot his father in the back, and waited for his mother to return home and shot her in the head while she was in the kitchen washing dishes. He told Hannaford that his father had repeatedly hit him on the head with a tool from his shed, and had called him 'Willy Lump Lump' because he had so many lumps on his head from the beatings. Eventually William could take no more of the violence and abuse and so he turned on his father. Interestingly, he remarked that if his father's guns had been locked up instead of being easily available, "it could have been a different story".

Neither Elliot Rodger, Jesse Osborne, nor Mark Barton had any difficulty in acquiring or using their guns for the purposes of mass shootings. Without guns, theirs might have been different stories too. But they would still have been stories of radical revenge, possibly with fewer fatalities, but shaped by a blind disregard for proportionality, intentionality and culpability.

Chapter Three
The Chilling World of Cyber Revenge

The internet offers an abundance of options for taking revenge, from cyberstalking, to trolling, to doxing, flaming, message bombing and so-called revenge porn. Even internet shopping provides new and outlandish possibilities, with websites that offer to deliver packages of faeces, bottles of urine or packets of pubic lice to the enemy of your choice. What makes online revenge particularly pernicious is that perpetrators need not be constrained by any sense of shame thanks to the anonymity that the internet provides, coupled with the ability of many users to split off their 'online self' from their so-called 'real self'. In the stories told in this chapter, the apparent shamelessness and relative effortlessness of taking radical online revenge is massively at odds with the devastating consequences it has for the victims.

Psychic processes associated with internet use

Although using the internet is in many ways a relatively passive occupation, it can also provide the user with a keen sense of agency. Once online, it is as easy to arrange a flower delivery as it is to destroy someone's credit rating, and as simple to apply for gym membership as to send someone a death threat. All it takes is a click or two. For people who may otherwise feel hopeless, marginalised or undervalued, this sense of potency can be especially important.

The feeling of power that can accompany online activity is bolstered by two other factors. First, there is something emboldening about knowing that one can escape instantaneously from an online exchange if it should become too challenging. The simple act of logging off makes it possible to avoid anticipated difficulties, and to enjoy the feeling of triumph that comes from the belief that the person at the other end of the exchange will feel frustrated and uncertain about what happened. Secondly, there is what the psychologist John Suler refers to as 'the online disinhibition effect' (Suler 2004). Sitting alone at the keyboard and using an online handle rather than a real name creates a feeling of anonymity, and a belief that nobody 'out there' will know what one is doing online. The conviction that there is no external authority to judge one's online actions can give free rein to acting out all sorts of pleasure-driven and primitive desires.

"On the Internet, nobody knows you're a dog."

The impact of the online disinhibition effect is well illustrated by the dramatic increase in the use of pornography since the internet became widely available. Prior to that, porn in the UK was accessible almost exclusively via specialist porn magazines. Purchasing a porn magazine was not always a simple process. The law stipulated that the magazines could only be displayed on newsagents' top shelves, a practice which reinforced the taboo attached to pornography at the time. The potential shame that would result from the newsagent and other customers knowing about one's proclivities was often enough to put off many would-be porn purchasers.

The taboo and shame that were once associated with using porn all but disappeared once internet porn became available. PornHub, the world's most heavily used pornography website, received globally on average 81 million hits *each day* in 2017, which is almost 4 million hits every hour (Castelman 2018). And PornHub is just one of many websites that cater to a range of tastes and tendencies. Ease of access has undoubtedly contributed to the exponential increase in online porn, and so too has the feeling of anonymity that online porn users can enjoy. The porn user no long has to be shamed at the newsagent's shop; instead, he can use any sort of porn at any time he chooses without anybody ever (seeming) to know what he is doing, or judge him for it (Cooper 2002).

But what about the judgement of an *internal* authority? While anonymity may quell anxieties about the disapproval of others, there is still the judgement of one's superego to contend with[11]. In many circumstances, the threat of the superego's disapprobation is enough to prevent people from acting on (or even letting themselves be consciously aware of) some of their darker wishes and urges. But for people who rely on the internet (and especially social media) for much of their social interaction, there is a tendency to split off what they do online from what they do 'in real life' (commonly known by the acronym IRL). As the online self becomes dissociated from what is thought of as the real self, the latter can remain responsive to the demands of conscience, while the online self is freed from these sorts of restrictions. At the same time, the online self can be distanced from aspects of the real self that the person may wish to

---

11 As Laplanche and Pontalis put it, "the super-ego's role in relation to the ego may be compared to that of a judge or a censor. Freud sees conscience, self-observation and the formation of ideals as functions of the super-ego" (Laplanche and Pontalis (1973).

disown (such as social awkwardness, loneliness, difficulties with body image, and other related feelings of inadequacy), and replaced by feelings of power and self-assurance.

For some people then, the internet provides a feeling of unfettered freedom and power. This arises out of a sort of magical thinking in which the unpleasantness of external reality is split off and disavowed in favour of a more pleasure-based, fantasied notion of reality (Ogden 2010). Over time, and depending on individual circumstances, the fantasies that are acted out in the cyber world become ever more compelling and feel increasingly 'real' for the individual, as was seen in the case of Jesse Osborne discussed in Chapter Two.

Most of us are susceptible to a degree of delusional thinking when we go online. When we read product reviews, we allow ourselves to believe that they were written by decent and trustworthy people like ourselves, rather than by a bot or by someone who was paid to write the review without ever having used the product. When we join a dating website we convince ourselves that what is in fact a perfect stranger is instead a perfect partner. When we send private information to someone in an email or direct message, we let ourselves believe that the only person ever to read the message will be the person for whom it is intended. These sorts of delusory thoughts are difficult to resist, but they are for the most part fleeting and harmless. However, in some cases the internet's fostering of delusion and magical thinking can have a more lasting impact on a person's way of thinking and being. The case of Elliot Rodger, discussed in Chapter Two, showed how a person who is consumed by grievance and resentment, and who has become socially and emotionally isolated, can be particularly vulnerable to internet dependency and addiction. Drawing on narcissistic defences, they may seek refuge from their real-life misery in the omnipotent fantasies of their online life.

The cyber world can hold a particular attraction for people who find intimacy disturbing but who at the same time feel unsafe when they are alone. As D.W.Winnicott explains, the capacity to be alone (in the deep sense of being at peace with one's self in its aloneness) depends on the person having been able to internalise the presence of someone who, in a very early stage of their development, was able to help them feel safe and peaceful (Winnicott 1958). Not all people have had this early experience and for those who have not, the feeling that they are alone can be a deeply disconcerting and even frightening experience of emptiness. In what is known as a core complex, the person draws away from a position of aloneness because it feels increasingly terrifying and unbearable, and moves instead towards closeness with another; this however soon becomes equally disturbing because of what feels increasingly like the risk of being engulfed or swallowed up by the other. And so there is a pull back to aloneness, which only offers temporary respite before the cycle begins again (Glasser 1985). With the arrival of the internet, a new pattern has emerged in which those who are locked in a core complex may develop a strong attachment to, and dependency on, online life which magically seems to provide a sort of closeness with others without involving any actual contact with them.

The psychic processes that are associated with internet use are important, not least because they enable people to move seamlessly from an *urge* for radical revenge to its *enactment*. While anonymity can free a person from the fear of being publicly shamed by their inappropriately extreme actions, the ability to split off the 'real self' from the cyber self helps to evade the judgements of one's conscience. Feelings of emptiness, unhappiness and uncertainty give way to a false sense of omnipotence and invincibility, while loneliness is replaced by a chimerical identification with an online 'community', as was the experience of Jesse Osborne.

The next three sections focus on three different areas of cyber-revenge: revenge porn, swatting, and trolling. What all three have in common is that the perpetrators generally operate with an assumption of invisibility and anonymity which gives them a feeling of power, and the shamelessness to say and do things they would probably never do IRL.

(i) Revenge porn

Revenge porn refers to the distribution of sexually explicit photos and footage without the consent of the person featured in the photos. The person may have been aware that the photos and videos were taken, but did not intend for the material to be distributed to others. In some cases, people are not even aware that intimate photos have been taken of them, and only find out once the photos are circulating online. In some of the most egregious cases of revenge porn, photos of rape and other non-consensual acts are posted online. In all cases, the distribution of the photos and videos is an act of aggression.

A number of commentators have argued that 'revenge porn' is a misnomer because not all cases of so-called revenge porn are motivated by revenge (Powell and Henry 2017). Although a number of alternative terms have been proposed such as non-consensual pornography and non-consensual image sharing, the term revenge porn is used in this chapter because the focus here is specifically on those cases of non-consensual sharing of photos that were explicitly motivated by the urge for radical revenge (Hall and Hearn 2018).

Those who are unfamiliar with the devastating consequences of revenge porn may be inclined to think of it as a relatively harmless practice which can cause mild embarrassment and maybe even some upset, but which cannot be said to constitute radical revenge in any real sense. This benign view is at odds with the findings of the Cyber Civil Rights Initiative whose survey showed that over 80% of respondents had experienced severe emotional distress and anxiety due to the dissemination of revenge porn (cited by Citron and Franks 2014). There are countless examples of the sheer devastation that revenge porn can cause. In a case described by Danielle Keats Citron, a woman's ex-partner posted her photo online, together with an advert saying she was interested in meeting "a real aggressive man with no concern for women". The ex-partner, who had placed the ad in the woman's name, was contacted by 160 men who expressed interest. He replied to one of the respondents and provided him with the woman's address. This man attacked the unsuspecting woman as she returned home, tied her up, blind-folded her, raped her, and abused her with a knife sharpener. Later, in his defence he said the woman had advertised for someone to rape her (Citron 2014). In another case, a 13-year-old schoolgirl was brutally attacked by a boy from her school who sodomised her, tried to rape her vaginally, and then shoved his penis in her mouth. The young girl was initially unable to tell anyone about the terrible trauma she had endured. She was unable to eat or sleep, she lost weight, and could not leave her room. When she eventually felt able to return to school she found that a video recording of the rape was circulating among her classmates. It transpired that the rapist had filmed the assault and was boasting of it to his school friends. As though the brutal attack had not been enough to bear, the young girl then had to face being taunted, laughed at and bullied by other children as the revenge porn did the rounds. Eventually the young girl had no choice but to ask for a transfer to another school (Goldberg 2019).

Revenge porn pre-dates the internet. In 1980 *Hustler* magazine introduced a competition in which it invited readers to send in images of naked women. Many of the photos that were submitted were of ex-partners. Although an unacceptable and aggressive violation of privacy, this early form of revenge porn had a fairly limited circulation. Conversely, victims of online revenge porn are left wondering for months and even years which of their friends, family, colleagues, neighbours and acquaintances are looking at their intimate photographs, which websites the photographs have been circulated on, and whether there is any way they can ever get the photographs taken down (Levendowski 2014). Legislators have begun to respond to pressure to introduce legal measures to punish perpetrators of revenge porn, but the legal challenges are considerable, and there is much work yet to be done. In the UK, the disclosure of intimate images or video without consent was made an offence in a 2018 update of the Criminal Justice and Courts Act 2015, but the fact that it is a communications offence rather than a sexual offence means that victims are likely to be publicly named during court proceedings which will inhibit many from taking the aggressor to court. In the US a number of states have existing civil laws (including copyright laws) which can be used to prosecute and punish revenge porn perpetrators. This is unfortunately of limited use because litigation is expensive and, even where it is pursued successfully, the existing laws cannot stop the spread of an image once it has been posted online (Citron and Franks 2014).

Although sometimes the revenge pornographer can profit financially from his actions by forcing his victim to pay to have the photos removed, more commonly the aim of revenge porn is to project feelings of shame, fear and vulnerability onto the victim, often in retaliation for having ended a relationship that left the ex-partner feeling rejected, humiliated and altogether diminished. According to a 2013 McAfee survey in the US, approximately 10% of ex-partners have threatened to post sexually explicit photos, and some 60% of those threats are subsequently carried out. In Britain, research carried out by the law firm Slater and Gordon showed that one in ten of their sample of 2000 respondents had had their naked photos or videos distributed without their consent. Of these, more than 80% knew the perpetrator, with a third having formerly been in a relationship with the person responsible.

Hunter Moore is widely known as 'the most hated man on the internet', an epithet given to him by *Rolling Stone* magazine in 2012. He gained notoriety by setting up one of the first revenge porn websites. In an hour-long YouTube interview with Dan Wise[12], Moore gave a glib explanation of how he came up with the idea of the website. As though to distance himself from its salaciousness, he said that "me and some friends just wanted to see a couple of girls we knew naked... and pretty quickly it went from a couple of friends to 40 to 70 million people looking at it per month" (YouTube 18 April 2018). Thousands of people sent him photos to post on his website. Many of these people were embittered ex-boyfriends and ex-husbands who sent in photos of their ex-partners in order to torment and shame them. To expand the website's reach further, Moore bought more naked photos from his collaborator, Charles Evens, who obtained them by hacking into women's email accounts and stealing the photos. Moore has been reviled, among other things for making money out of this perverse arrangement by charging victims a fee to take their pictures down from the website. He revelled in his infamy,

---

12 Dan Wise is a federal prison coach whom Hunter had consulted prior to serving a prison sentence. A prison coach, or prison consultant, provides advice to people who have received a custodial sentence on how to survive and cope with prison conditions.

narcissistically cultivating it via television and newspaper interviews and social media.

What is often overlooked, and rarely mentioned by Moore himself, is that he was initially motivated to start thinking in terms of 'revenge' porn by feelings of loss and shame that were too difficult for him to bear. Although he implied when speaking with Dan Wise that it all started as a bit of hi-jinks with friends who "just wanted to see a couple of girls we knew naked", in a shorter and distinctly less polished interview in 2012 Moore let slip that:

> ... it all started with, erm...well you know. Me hating some dumb
> bitch who broke my heart really. And that's how it started, dude.
> Trying to get back at somebody and revenge, basically. For fucking
> with me and I wanted to fuck with them ten times harder.
> (YouTube 28 July 2012)

In response to having his heart broken, and evidently feeling diminished and ashamed that his girlfriend had rejected and him, he not only wanted to pay her back, he wanted to 'fuck with her ten times harder': an unambiguous statement of disproportionality.

Hunter Moore is just one of the many thousands of men around the world who have posted revenge porn online as a way of retaliating against an ex-partner. What these men share is a (usually unconscious) fantasy that they can somehow shed their terrible sense of shame and grievance by inflicting these painful feelings onto their ex-partner. The need to project their feelings is especially intense in thin-skinned narcissists who cannot bear the shame, and the wound to their sense of self, when a woman wants to end a relationship with them.

The case of Shawn Sayer illustrates how obsessive and delusional this form of revenge can be. Sayer was in a romantic relationship for three years with a woman who is referred to in court documents by the fictitious name, Jane Doe. Shortly after Jane Doe broke up with Sayer in January 2006, Sayer began stalking and harassing her. Initially, he turned up at shops and other venues where he knew he would find her. She responded to this intimidation by changing her routine and giving up activities that she had previously enjoyed so as to avoid seeing Sayer. As the stalking continued, she eventually obtained a protection order against Sayer in the State Court. Two years later, still harbouring his grievance against Jane Doe, Sayer began to use the internet to harass and threaten her. He set up a Facebook account in her name and posted naked photos of her, giving details of her address with the message that she was looking for "sexual entertainment". She was terrified when several unknown men turned up at her house offering to provide what the fake Facebook account had claimed she was looking for. The Facebook account was just one of many attempts to terrorise Jane Doe. Sayer also placed an ad in her name on Craigslist, with pictures of her in her underwear which he had taken when they were together. The ad provided details of how to get to her house, and information on the sexual acts that she was purportedly willing to perform. In 2009, Jane Doe changed her name and moved to another state to live with her aunt in order to escape Sayer's harassment. Feeling protected by her new identity, she began a new career and felt safe for a short time, until she was approached by a strange man who said he had met her online. It transpired that Sayer had posted on pornographic websites a number of videos of Sayer and Jane Doe engaging in sexual acts, videos that had been filmed while they were dating. Once again, her address had been provided to anyone wishing to meet her. She eventually returned to her home state because her aunt had become so frightened of the strange men appearing at her home at all times of day or night. Sayer was finally arrested in July 2010 for violating a protective order, and in July 2011 he was indicted on one count of cyber-stalking and one count of identity theft. Sayer had turned to the internet to get revenge on his ex-partner, committing a number of criminal offences in the process. And yet after more than four years of stalking, harassing and 'punishing' his ex-partner, he remained unable to rid himself of the feelings of grievance that had been evoked by the ending of their relationship.

(ii) Swatting

Special Weapons and Tactics (SWAT) teams are US police units that are trained to use military manoeuvres in response to highly dangerous emergency situations. In recent years SWAT teams have been used as pawns in online conflicts and rivalries. The practice, which has come to be known as swatting, involves making a prank phone call to the police, falsely claiming that a highly dangerous event is under way at the unsuspecting victim's address, and thereby prompting an unnecessary emergency response by the police SWAT team. Swatting is increasingly used as a form of revenge among the gaming community where riled players swat their opponents' homes. In addition to being a complete waste of police time, swatting can have devastating consequences for those involved.

The US Federal Bureau of Investigation (FBI) estimates that 400 swatting incidents occur annually, and the trend seems to be on the increase. In 2015 Representative Katherine Clark of Massachusetts sponsored the Interstate Swatting Hoax Act in the House of Representatives, making it a federal crime to provoke an emergency response by any US law enforcement agency without just cause. A few months later, a hoax call to her local police station resulted in Representative Clark's house being swarmed by a SWAT team. Representative Clark assumed that she had been swatted in retaliation for having sponsored the Act. This was a reasonable assumption, given that a similar incident had occurred a few months earlier, when New Jersey Assemblyman Paul Moriarty was swatted, apparently in retaliation for having sponsored an anti-swatting Bill aimed at increasing penalties for raising 'false public alarm'. One evening when Moriarty was at home he received a phone call from a police officer who asked if he was alright because they had just been informed there had been a shooting in his house. Looking out of his window, he saw six police cars outside his home, with officers in helmets and flak jackets, all carrying rifles.

Although neither Katherine Clark nor Paul Moriarty were physically hurt in these incidents, the experience will at the very least have caused them some anxiety. In other cases, the consequences are even more severe and can include serious injuries and even fatalities. Police who attend a scene where a potentially deadly crime is reported will be under intense pressure and on high alert, expecting to encounter armed and dangerous criminals. Where police and many civilians carry guns, as they do in the US, this sort of situation can be perilous. Just as the police attending the alleged crime scene are on edge, so too the ordinary law-abiding citizen who has been swatted can assume that the people suddenly surrounding their house are dangerous, and the citizen may brandish a firearm in what they believe is self-defence. The result can be a quick escalation of violence with tragic consequences.

What does this have to do with cyber-revenge? Swatting has been the weapon of choice for many cyber-bullies and harassers as well as others seeking revenge in online conflicts. Swatting, like much revenge that is perpetrated online, is carried out anonymously. Calls are made to the police using disguised voices and fake identities. The swatter's victim will usually have a good idea of who the perpetrator is, but nobody else will, and even the victim will be hard pressed to prove beyond doubt who the perpetrator was. Undoubtedly this anonymity contributes to the use of swatting as a tool of revenge for those who spend many of their waking hours engaged in online activities.

Swatting was one of the weapons of choice used by the notorious online movement known as Gamergate. This loose but powerful movement targeted gamers with progressive views and, in particular, female gamers who were regarded by many male gamers as an unwanted presence in the world of gaming. One male gamer, who went by the online handle of 'Obnoxious', routinely harassed female gamers on the popular gaming website Twitch and when his targets refused to acquiesce to the demand that they leave or reduce their presence in the gaming community, he threatened to swat them. In one case, a young female college student who ignored Obnoxious's online attacks and threats was woken one night by her panicked father who told her to come downstairs immediately. Doing as she was told, she was terrified to see at least five police officers in full riot gear, guns drawn. Another swatting victim who had ignored warnings from Gamergate trolls received a phone call telling her to step outside of her house with her hands above her head. She later described it as the most terrifying experience of her life (Fagone 2015).

The use of swatting in the pursuit of radical revenge is exemplified in the 2017 case of two (male) gamers who became embroiled in a conflict while playing the online game, *Call of Duty World War II*. One of the players was 18-year-old Casey Viner from North College Hill, Ohio; the other was 19-year-old Shane Gaskill of Wichita, Kansas. Viner and Gaskill were playing on the same side (from different locations) in a four-versus-four game of *Call of Duty* on a site that allowed gamers to play for money. Viner and Gaskill's team had lost the match as well as a wager, in part because Gaskill had inadvertently 'killed' Viner's character in a 'friendly fire incident'. An argument then developed online between Viner and Gaskill, with Viner furious that Gaskill had cost the team their important win. Enraged by the loss, Viner contacted 25-year-old Tyler Barriss to help him get revenge on Gaskill.

Barriss had gained notoriety in the gaming community through his experience with swatting. He had been involved in Gamergate swatting, having targeted (among others) the well-known Canadian gamer, Lisa Bannatta. Known on Twitter by his handle @SWAuTistic, Barriss agreed to swat Gaskill on behalf of Viner. Barriss began checking Gaskill's Twitter account to see if he could identify the address he would later send the police to. However, Gaskill became aware that Barriss was stalking him, and quickly worked out that Viner had arranged for him to be swatted. Thinking he was one step ahead of his opponent, Gaskill began to send provocative messages to Barriss, as though to encourage the swatting. Gaskill even gave Barriss his home address – except, crucially, it was an old address where he and his family no longer lived.

Barriss duly called the police and gave them the address that Gaskill had provided him with, telling the emergency services that he was at that address and he had just shot his father in the head and was going to kill his mother and brother. The SWAT team rushed to the address Barriss had provided, where the resident was completely unaware of what had been going on. The resident, Andrew Finch, heard a noise outside his house and stepped out onto the porch. He was immediately blinded by the bright police lights that were directed onto him. He complied with the order to raise his hands, but he then lowered one arm to his waist, possibly to tighten his belt. As he did so, a police officer mistakenly thought Finch was reaching for a gun and immediately shot Finch, killing the 28-year-old father who had not played any role in the conflict of which he was a victim.

Barriss was sentenced to 20 years in prison after pleading guilty to more than 50 swatting-related crimes. Viner was sentenced to 15 months for his role in the swatting incident that had resulted in the death of Andrew Finch. At the time of writing, Gaskill is still waiting for sentencing. Viner's desire for retaliation against Gaskill had been provoked by his rage and shame at having lost a *Call of Duty* game and lost the wager linked to the game. The amount of money he had lost was less than $2, a loss that would have felt trivial in 'real life', but which had enraged Viner's online self. He hoped that by swatting Gaskill he would be able to restore his wounded pride and sense of self.

What is interesting is that when Viner found out that his actions had led to the death of an innocent man, he seemed bewildered and panicked, as though the bringing together of his 'real self' and his 'online self' was disorienting in some way. Shortly after he heard about the killing of Andrew Finch, Viner sent his friend a link to a news story about the shooting and asked the friend, "if [i]t's on those websites, does that mean it's real?" His friend, perhaps recognising Viner's confusion between reality and online fantasy, replied that the story of the shooting did not seem "related to game stuff". A short while later the friend texted, "hopefully you didn't say anything stupid". Viner replied "I did, I literally said you're gonna be swatted. *Not thinking at all*, so I'm going to prison." (my italics) (United States District Court, District of Kansas, Case no. 18-100765).

This tragic story that ended in an innocent man's death highlights how absorption in the online world can lead to a state of 'not thinking at all', which in turn can facilitate the move from *wanting* revenge to *taking* revenge, without any thought to the likely consequences. At his sentencing, Viner trembled as he told the court that he was very sorry and that he had "never intended for anything to happen".

(iii) Trolling

Trolling involves posting online comments (and sometimes pictures) that aim to offend, upset, or terrorise other internet users. The comments range from the mildly provocative to something altogether more sinister and disturbing, including death and rape threats. Trolls target people for their views, their successes or failures, their likes or dislikes, their appearance, their occupations, or indeed any other feature that the troll chooses to pick on. Hardaker suggests that trolling is sometimes carried out to alleviate boredom, while ethnographer Whitney Phillips found in her research that trolls are often searching for what is called lulz[13], which is essentially amusement at someone else's expense (Hardaker 2013; Phillips 2015). While many agree that trolls derive pleasure from annoying, upsetting, or hurting their victims, what is sometimes overlooked is that often this pleasure relates to the radical revenge involved in much trolling. Even though 'in real life' the troll may not know their victim, they may feel the need to retaliate for feelings of envy or shame which the victim has unwittingly and unintentionally provoked in the troll. Trolling is a widespread form of radical revenge because the troll feels safe in the belief that their victims do not know the troll's 'real life' identity, and so the victim will have little opportunity for effective comeback.

The trolling of Andy Woodward, a former professional English footballer, illustrates how devastating it is to be the target of online revenge which takes no account of intentionality or culpability. Like most professional footballers, Woodward started training at a young age and gained experience by playing for a number of youth football teams. Between the ages of 11 and 17, Woodward was sexually and emotionally abused by his football coach, Barry Bennell, who manipulated and terrorised Woodward into remaining silent about the abuse while it was going on and for many years afterwards. Outwardly a successful football player, Woodward struggled for years with feelings of despair and thoughts of suicide. He experienced panic attacks, developed a drink problem and had an eating disorder. His personal relationships suffered, and he often felt on edge. When other men began to come forward to accuse Bennell of child sexual abuse, Woodward felt able to give evidence in court. In doing this he helped to convict Bennell. At this stage Woodward's identity was kept private and few people outside his innermost circle knew what he had been through. Eventually, in November 2016, at the age of 43 and with his

---

13 Lulz derives from the slang term 'lol'(laugh out loud).

football career long past, Andy Woodward decided to step forward to tell the world openly and publicly about what had happened to him. He rightly believed that there were many others who had been horribly abused by Barry Bennell, and that many more would continue to suffer at the hands of paedophiles if the truth were not told. Although speaking out cost Woodward a great deal in terms of having to revisit difficult memories, in doing this he cleared the way for hundreds of other men and boys to come forward with their own painful accounts of having been abused by youth football coaches (Woodward 2019).

Within two days of telling the world his story, Andy Woodward received a message on Twitter from an account in the name of 'The Nonce' (a slang term for paedophile). The Twitter account holder's profile picture was of Bennell. The message read: "Hi Andy. Am feeling horny. Fancy popping round mine?", and was accompanied by a cartoon-like video clip of Bennell sucking a lollipop. When he read the troll's message, Woodward felt physically sick. He dropped his phone and collapsed. A family member had to hold him up to prevent him from falling onto the floor. Woodward was immediately transported back to the terrors of his childhood, and felt frightened, vulnerable and powerless (Taylor 2017). Having already been diagnosed with post-traumatic stress disorder, after receiving the Twitter message he was prescribed medication to manage the painful feelings and flashbacks that haunted him.

Partly because of the publicity surrounding Woodward's case, extensive efforts were made to trace the troll who had sent him the odious message. The troll was eventually identified and taken to court where he received a 12-month prison sentence together with a 15-year restraining order. He turned out to be a teenage boy from Crewe in the northwest of England. The 18-year-old perpetrator initially convinced his father to take the blame, but eventually admitted that he was the one who had sent the messages to Woodward.

Why would this young man attack Andy Woodward in this way? Was it simply a matter of boredom or a search for 'lulz'? During his police interview the perpetrator said, "I was so bitter about my own life I thought I would try to upset somebody else's", indicating that his act had been a form of radical revenge against someone who seemed better off. Perhaps the troll envied Woodward his football skills or – more likely – he envied Woodward's bravery in speaking up about a traumatic experience, a bravery which the youngster perhaps wished he himself had. The troll described himself as being "not right in the head" because of "a number of personal issues", and because he had recently lost his job. Disturbed and aggrieved, the perpetrator wanted radical revenge, and Woodward had the terrible misfortune of being associated in the perpetrator's mind with his shame and anger.

Another dramatic example of how radical revenge can be played out through trolling is seen in the experience of the writer and performer Lindy West. What sets West's story apart from many others is the way she responded to one of the trolls who targeted her, and the insight which their exchange provides into the link between trolling and the desire for radical revenge.

Lindy West is a feminist writer who has contributed to *The Guardian*, *The New York Times*, *GQ*, and *Jezebel.com*. Describing herself as a fat woman, she has often written about body-image and fat-shaming. In her book, *Shrill: Notes from a Loud Woman*, she explains that although many people stare at her, laugh at her, and criticise her for being fat, she feels comfortable and empowered by her body.

West recounts the conflict she had with her boss over his repeated public disparagement of fat people. After failing to convince him that his comments were unnecessarily hurtful, she wrote in a private email to him, "on top of the trolls who call me a fat cunty virgin every day of my life, now I also get trolls asking me, 'How does it feel to know your boss thinks you're a disgusting cow?'" (West, 2017). Despite her pleas, her boss's public mockery of fat people continued. West eventually decided to respond to him publicly. She posted her photograph online with details of her height and weight, accompanied by a description of herself in which she stated:

This is my body. It is MINE. I am not ashamed of it in any way. In fact, I love everything about it. Men find it attractive. Clothes look awesome on it. My brain rides around in it all day and comes up with funny jokes. Also, I don't have to justify its awesomeness/ attractiveness/healthiness/usefulness to anyone, because it is MINE. Not yours. (West 2017, p.99)

This forthright description of herself as a fat person who is comfortable with her own body image was the first of West's many bold public statements on the subject of being a fat woman.

Another subject she tackled was the unacceptability of so-called 'rape jokes' which numerous male comedians continue to use in their stand-up routines. In 2013 West was invited by the US television show *Totally Biased* to debate the issue of 'rape jokes' with a popular male comedian. During the debate, West argued that there is never anything funny about rape, while her opponent insisted that 'they're just jokes'.

The online fall-out began to unfold two days later. West received a slew of messages on Twitter, Facebook, YouTube and email to the effect that she was too fat and ugly for anyone ever to want to rape her. She was described as "about as fun as dry rape", and was advised "Kill yourself, dumb bitch". According to West, there were hundreds and hundreds of other toxic messages that felt like an "unyielding wall of vitriol" (West 2017). The experience, she says, was like "drowning and falling all at once". However, rather than drop her argument, West continued to speak out against a culture that condones so-called 'rape jokes'.

The trolling continued too. In the same year that she had spoken out against 'rape jokes', West received strange messages from a Twitter account purportedly belonging to her beloved father who had died eighteen months previously. The Twitter account featured a photograph of West's father, and was in a name that was a distortion of her father's name, with a bio that said he was the "embarrassed father of an idiot".

West was unsure whether and how to respond to this, and to the hundreds of other hate-filled messages. She thought she should stop reading the trolls' attacks, but at the same time she felt she had to continue looking through them in order to know whether anyone who was targeting her online might actually present a threat to her safety. She wondered if she should stop writing about contentious subjects so as to avoid the trolls' ire, but she could not countenance being silenced in this way. After some deliberation, she decided on a different course of action. She wrote an article on the feminist website *Jezebel.com* about the experience of having been trolled by someone who had pretended to be her father. She wrote an honest account of how much it had hurt her. And then, as West later said in a radio interview, "something amazing happened" (This American Life 2015). West received an email the following day from the troll who had set up an account in the name of her dead father. He said that he did not really know why he had attacked her, and that in fact he agreed with her that 'rape jokes' are not funny. Apologising for what he had done, he wrote: "I think my anger towards you stems from your happiness with your own being. It offended me because it served to highlight my unhappiness with my own self." He explained that when he read what West had written on *Jezebel.com*, he realised that "there is a living, breathing human being who is reading this shit. I am attacking someone who never harmed me in any way." He apologised again, and told West that he had made a $50 donation to the cancer charity which had supported West's father.

This was an unexpected outcome which sheds some light on what was behind the troll's attack on Lindy West. Something about West's self-assuredness had filled him with such terrible envy that he wanted to punish her. He felt he had to project his own unhappiness and desperation onto her by attacking her and leaving her feeling weak and vulnerable, and himself feeling (temporarily) strong and powerful. West received just one more email from the troll, apologising again and giving her his real name. She heard no more from him, but a few months later West decided she needed a better understanding of what had made the troll do what he had done to her. She approached him via the US radio programme *This American Life* whose producers contacted the troll to ask if he would be willing to speak on the phone with Lindy West about what had happened. They explained that the phone conversation would be recorded, and clips would then be broadcast on an episode of *This American Life*. The troll agreed to the request.

The show, which was broadcast in early 2015, combined West's reflections on her encounter with the troll with a number of clips from the telephone conversation which had lasted over two hours. As before, the troll told West that he did not object to her stance on 'rape jokes', but what had enraged him was West writing about how proud she is of herself, and her contentment with her life. At the time of his attacks on West, he explained, he was at a low point in his own life: he hated his body, which he felt was 75 pounds overweight; his girlfriend had ended their relationship; and he was stuck in an unfulfilling job. Filled with shame and grievance, he was overcome by envy and resentment towards Lindy West who seemed comfortable with her body and her life. He sought respite by attacking her online, not only through the fake Twitter account, but through a host of other vicious comments he had posted prior to setting up the account.

How can the troll's turnaround, from mercilessly attacking West to asking for her forgiveness, be accounted for? The troll himself admitted that when he was attacking Lindy West through the fake Twitter account, he had lost any awareness that she was a real person who had thoughts and feelings like him. There is not much scope – or need – for empathy when the person you are attacking is not a 'real' person, but just a name or image on the screen. When West wrote about the impact of the troll's actions on her, and described the hurt he had caused her, he began to realise that the target of his venom was a real person who had suffered the loss of her much-loved father. With this realisation came a deep sense of shame for his actions, which in turn led him to apologise. Not everyone would have responded to shame in this way; many people would have continued trying to project it rather than face up to it. The case is an interesting one, not least because it demonstrates how powerful shame can be in triggering, but *also* putting a brake on radical revenge.

Another successful, confident woman who has been targeted relentlessly by trolls is the eminent classicist Professor Mary Beard. Ironically, one of her areas of research concerns the different ways that men throughout the ages have tried to silence outspoken women. Beard is a prolific writer and captivating speaker both on radio and television. She has brought the classical world to life for many listeners, and engages with a wide audience on social media. Yet for all her achievements, her detractors have chosen to focus on her age, her gender and her physical appearance, suggesting that by these standards she is unwanted and should remain silent. On one occasion, after one of her television programmes had aired, a well-known critic wrote in the *Sunday Times* that Mary Beard was too old and too ugly to present a history programme on television. Beard replied in an article in the *Daily Mail* entitled, *'Too Ugly for TV? No, I'm too Brainy for Men Who Fear Clever Women.'*

This was not the only time Beard was crudely attacked. In 2013 she received an abusive message on Twitter in which the troll called her a "filthy old slut" and commented on her genitalia. Beard retweeted his message to her many thousands of Twitter followers. They responded with expressions of outrage, and one tweeted back to Beard (and to all who were reading Beard's Twitter account) saying they knew who the culprit was, and offering to send her the contact details of the troll's mother. Within a few minutes, the troll – who turned out to be a 20-year-old university student – wrote to apologise to Beard, calling himself "wrong and very rude". In a BBC radio interview a short time later, Beard talked about being trolled and said that most people who are trolled are advised not to react, and instead just to ignore it. However, her retweeting of the troll's cruel message – and the possibility of his mother finding out about what he had done – had a profound effect on the troll. Like the man who had attacked Lindy West, this young man had to face up to the reality of his online actions, and in the process he was shamed into apologising for his delinquent behaviour.

Radical revenge: gender and misogyny

This chapter has looked at just three areas of internet revenge: revenge porn, swatting and trolling. While it is clear that most cases of revenge porn and swatting are carried out by men, it is more difficult to assess the gender split in trolling because most trolls keep their 'real life' identities so well-hidden. However, when all forms of internet abuse are taken together under the one category of cyber-harassment, studies suggest that men are significantly more likely to be the perpetrators. A study carried out in New

York for the FBI Law Enforcement Bulletin found that 80% of people who had been reported to have caused "aggravated harassment" online were men (D'Ovidio and Doyle 2003), and this is supported by Donner's more recent study of 522 college students which found that men were more likely to engage in cyber-harassment than women (Donner 2016). Karla Mantilla, who researched what she calls gendertrolling, observes that "Regardless of the few women who do join in gendertrolling campaigns, the vastly overwhelming majority of participants are men." (Mantilla 2015). In view of findings such as these, and given that 95% of mass shootings in the US were perpetrated by men as noted in Chapter Two, it seems essential to give some thought to the significance of gender in radical revenge.

A good starting point is the work of Gina Rippon, a cognitive neuroscientist who has studied neurological responses to experiences of rejection (referred to in her work as rejection-sensitivity). The evidence indicates that while aggression is a common response to rejection in both men and women, there are interesting gender differences in the ways that the aggression tends to be expressed. Rippon found that women were more likely to have "adverse 'internalising' responses associated with depression" when faced with rejection, a reaction which generally resulted in behaviours described as self-silencing. Conversely, men were much more likely to externalise their responses to rejection by behaving aggressively towards others rather than towards themselves.

How can we account for these gendered differences in responses to emotionally difficult experiences? Rippon disputes the idea that they are due to inherent or immutable differences in women's and men's brains, and instead points to the plasticity of the brain, and to the way that our brains change in response to the acquisition of different experiences, and exposure to different expectations of others and of themselves. The same, she says, is true of hormone levels which are driven not only by biology but also by the sorts of activities that a person is engaged with, and by their expectations. She points to the lower levels of testosterone found in men who spend larger amounts of time caring for their children compared to fathers who spend less time caring for their children. This raises questions of causality, which Rippon duly addresses. Interestingly, the difference in hormone levels is found not only between individual men who may or may not choose to spend relatively large amounts of time looking after their children, but also between groups of men. Rippon refers for instance to a study of two different groups in Tanzania: in the group where the cultural norm was for fathers to care for their young, testosterone levels were lower than in the group where this was not the norm, suggesting that caring for children is not a function of comparatively low testosterone, but rather the other way around (Rippon 2019).

The intractable question of nature versus nurture remains wide open but what is unarguable is that there are deeply embedded social influences and cultural practices in contemporary developed societies which help to determine, and reinforce, the disparity in the ways that aggression – and the urge for revenge – are expressed by men and women. As the journalist Caitlin Dewey observes, "Even 'good guys' learn from childhood that 'throwing like a girl' is bad, and that the man in a relationship always 'wears the pants'" (Dewey 2015). Crucially, the deeply embedded social norms that make even the 'good guys' want to show themselves and the rest of the world that they are the ones who 'wear the pants' form a critical influence on the gendered nature of radical revenge.

This chapter raises a further question regarding gender which is to do with the *targets* of cyber-revenge (and perhaps of radical revenge more generally). Women are undoubtedly the victims of the vast majority of revenge porn cases, but it is more difficult to establish the gender balance among victims of cyber harassment more widely. Small-scale studies such as D'Ovidio and Doyle's suggest that women account for significantly more reported cases of cyber harassment than men, but their evidence is too limited to be generalisable (D'Ovidio and Doyle 2003). While it is difficult to be precise about numbers, what is clear is that much of the cyber-revenge aimed at women is overtly sexualised and misogynistic, and often focusses on female genitalia and other body parts. How, if at all, does this relate to radical revenge?

Much of the material discussed in this chapter has shown that women are often targeted for radical revenge because they have in some way diminished the (male) aggressor's feelings of masculinity and potency. This often occurs when a woman has the temerity to end a relationship, leaving her ex-partner feeling shamed by feelings of rejection. The ex-partner may turn to stalking, revenge porn, trolling – or other forms of abuse and violence – in an effort to project their painful feelings onto the woman in revenge for what she has done, as was the case with Hunter Moore and Shawn Sayer.

A second reason that women may become the target of a man's radical revenge is that they have succeeded in getting themselves noticed and heard in ways which make some men feel neglected or inadequate. This was evidently the experience of the troll who targeted Lindy West in retaliation for her strident comments online and in the mass media. When West later asked the troll if his anger at her outspokenness was to do with her being a woman, he replied: "Oh, definitely. Definitely. Women are being more forthright in their writing. You know, they're not – there isn't a sense of timidity to when they speak or when they write. They're saying it loud. And I think that – and I think – for me, as well – it's threatening at first" (This American Life 2015). The list of women who have been targeted for speaking up is a long one, and includes authors, politicians, activists and actors. Many more of the victims of trolling do not have celebrity status and they bear the harassment, threats and bullying outside of the limelight. There is of course a small minority of women who troll other women for speaking up, but in the vast majority of cases the perpetrators are men.

A third and related reason that a woman may become the victim of a man's radical revenge is that she has bettered him in some way, leaving him feeling envious and aggrieved. Danielle Keats Citron describes the experience of a young female law student who, shortly after being declared one of the top performers in a competition between law schools, read online comments from other students such as "I think I will sodomize her. Repeatedly" and "Clearly she deserves to be raped so that her little fantasy world can be shattered by real life" (Citron 2014). The case of Mark Barton which was discussed in Chapter Two provides another example of a man taking radical revenge against a woman because she had succeeded where he had failed. Barton brutally murdered his second wife because he could not bear the ignominy and humiliation of having had to depend on her for the shelter which he had failed to provide for himself and his children.

A fourth reason that women are targeted is that they have not made themselves available for the trolls' sexual desires[14]. The case of Elliot Rodger described in Chapter Two, and the 'incel' (involuntary celibate) movement which he inspired, are examples of this (Manne 2019). The delusional thinking that defines the incel movement is summed up in posts such as these which are taken from the website reddit.com:

> We are the superior gender. We're taller, stronger, smarter, if each of us played 'eeny meeny miny moe' and picked a girl to beat up/rape/kill, we could. No question.

> Swallow a handful of Cialis [a medication commonly used to treat erectile dysfunction] so you have a boner all night long, then destroy that pussy, turn her brown eye blue, and blow your spunk all over her uvula [sic]. And the next morning she won't remember a damned thing.

> Unless women are controlled they will act like parasites towards vulnerable men.

This belief that women are lesser beings who should be controlled by men – and that they should not make themselves heard, should not excel, and indeed should not do anything which diminishes a man's sense of maleness and power – is widely known as misogyny. It is suggested here that acting on misogynistic beliefs is a form of radical revenge against women for not fulfilling the role which misogynists expect them to fill. This expected role is in essence that of the ever-present (yet somehow also silent and invisible) woman who can magically meet the physical, sexual

---

14 There is a degree of speciousness here, however, because the women who *are* regarded as 'available' are attacked for being 'sluts' and 'whores'.

and emotional needs of the misogynist in such a way that he does not even have to experience the shame of needing her.

This brings to mind Donald Winnicott's conception of early infant development. In the first few weeks of life, the infant is not yet aware of the 'otherness' of his mother; he does not see her as a being which is separate from him. In this early phase of her infant's life, the good enough mother will be absorbed in what Winnicott refers to as 'primary maternal preoccupation'. In this state, she will be able to sense and pre-empt most of the young infant's needs, and will feed him and tend to him *before* he becomes painfully aware of unmet needs. But this early phase of meeting the infant's every need is relatively short-lived. With healthy development must come the baby's slow realisation that mother is *sometimes* there to meet his needs, *but not always*. In other words, he learns to accept, slowly but surely, a painful piece of reality, namely that mother is not the infant's omnipotently controlled object: she is a separate being who cares for him but who also has interests and preoccupations other than him. This idea of separateness develops gradually, and with it comes an ability to tolerate frustration and a new (and more mature) way of relating to mother (and others) (Winnicott 1969). The vengeful misogynist seems to have missed this phase of development. He is unable to come to terms with any frustration of his needs and wants, and is equally unable to think of women as anything other than body parts which exist purely for his gratification.

There is a further parallel to be drawn. A hungry or lonely infant may comfort himself by sucking his thumb or finger, but this hallucinated comfort can only be temporary, and soon will give way to the real feelings of hunger or loneliness. Similarly, the misogynist troll may seek comfort by projecting his feelings of vulnerability, shame and envy onto women, but any comfort that derives from this projection can only be short-lived; soon enough, the feelings of envy and of shame return. This helps to explain why many trolls and revenge pornographers feel the need to continue posting long strings of vindictive messages over days, weeks and even years, hoping for a more permanent relief that can never be achieved through magical thinking.

The Chilling World of Cyber Revenge

Misogyny is often referred to as the world's oldest prejudice. It has certainly been around for many centuries. In today's world the internet provides new and seemingly endless opportunities for unbridled expressions of misogyny. These opportunities relate in part to the opening up of new channels of communication; but as this chapter has shown, they also relate to the complex psychic processes associated with internet use. For many people, what may once have been a wish for radical revenge can now be shamelessly converted into acts of radical revenge, often with dire consequences for victims and perpetrators alike.

Chapter Four
Groups and Radical Revenge

Aggrieved individuals are often more inclined to act on their urge for radical revenge when they are part of a group that shares their grievances and their desire for payback. Swayed by the group's suggestions, feeling less exposed by virtue of being just one of many and, perhaps most important of all, galvanised by a powerful leader, disgruntled individuals will allow themselves to be drawn in to the group's acts of radical revenge. These acts can range from covert acts of sabotage, to violent one-off attacks, to military reprisals, to more structured political programmes of revenge, but in all cases they are undertaken without regard for proportionality, intentionality or culpability. This chapter begins by looking more closely at how an individual can be swept up by the group's calls for radical revenge, and moves on to focus on one particular case: the consistent targeting by President Trump and his followers of minority groups in revenge for social and economic difficulties which they had not in fact caused.

Individuals and Groups

In his 1921 paper *Group Psychology and the Analysis of the Ego*, Sigmund Freud draws attention to the fact that when an individual becomes part of a group, he adjusts his thoughts and feelings to bring them more in line with those of other group members. Freud suggests that what is central to this process of adjustment and conformity is the individual's identification with other group members. For Freud, identification is the key to group cohesion, and is understood to arise out of a psychic connection between people that is based on a perceived quality of sameness. This sameness may be in the realm of a shared culture, shared interests, shared beliefs and values, or shared grievances (the latter of which has particular relevance in cases of group revenge). The more value an individual places on the shared qualities, the greater their sense of identification with the group. And the greater the identification, the stronger the inclination to keep in step with the group by saying, doing and sometimes even thinking things that he may not have (consciously) countenanced as a lone individual. This is as true of the school child who wears outlandish clothes in order to conform to his friendship group as it is of the soldier who joins his brother-in-arms in committing heinous war crimes that as an individual he would have condemned. For Freud, the tendency to go along with the group is ultimately "an irreducible, primitive phenomenon, a fundamental fact in the mental life of man" (Freud 1921, p.89).

Part of what makes the individual open to the group's suggestions, and so willing to conform to the thoughts and actions of other group members, is the desire to preserve his place within the group. For many, group membership brings feelings of security, stability and identity. Where compromise and conformity are called for, they will often be conceded in order to be able to stay within the group rather than be pushed out of it. One of Freud's contemporaries, Ernst Kris, offered a further explanation for our proclivity to follow the group's suggestion. He argued that the power of suggestion depends on the extent to which the thing that is being suggested by the group corresponds with the individual's conscious *and unconscious* wishes (Kris 1941). The greater the correspondence, the greater the sense of gratification that derives from going along with what is being suggested. While an individual might doubt the soundness or rectitude of the group's suggestions, these doubts can be disavowed, denied or otherwise defended against in favour of the group's suggestions, where these suggestions gratify the individual's unconscious desires.

One of the most compelling illustrations of the power of suggestion can be found in Christopher Browning's remarkable book, *Ordinary Men*. Browning analysed what happened when in 1942 a unit of almost 500 'ordinary' middle aged German reservists were ordered by their leader, Major Trapp, to round up the 1,800 Jews living in the Polish village of Józefów, and to shoot all of the women, children and men, sparing only those who could be useful in labour camps. When Major Trapp announced the plan for this attack he offered every member of the battalion the chance to opt out of the massacre if they felt unable to go ahead with it. Only a dozen of the almost 500 men took up this offer. The rest proceeded with the slaughter.

Why would this group of ordinary men be so willing and able to engage in such a horrific act of brutality? Using records of interrogations that took place after the attack, Browning found little evidence that the men were (consciously) motivated by anti-Semitism or sadism when they agreed to join in with the attack[15]. Instead, some explained that they had gone along with the attack because it was all such a rush, and they felt they hadn't been given enough time to consider the possibility of opting out. In other words, in the absence of time to think and reflect, the immediate reaction of these men was to go along with what the leader and the other men were doing, rather than take a stand against it. How can this be explained?

Thinking back to Ernst Kris's argument, one might reasonably speculate that going along with General Trapp's planned attack satisfied the unconscious wishes and desires of at least some of the men. It is, however, not possible to establish whether, or to what extent, this was the case. What does emerge from the evidence is that many of the men were consciously swayed by their desire to protect and uphold their ties with the group. Reviewing the interrogation records, Browning notes the importance of "the basic identification of men in uniform with their comrades and the strong urge not to separate themselves from the group by stepping out" (Browning 1992). In short, many of the men were willing to engage in the slaughter in order to protect and uphold their valued bond with the group. To do otherwise would risk being regarded as a coward, treated as an outsider and, as a consequence, losing the valued security of being part of the group.

---

15 Browning does note however that, despite the absence of explicit anti-Semitism among those who were interrogated, it was clear that the men had taken in the idea that 'the Jews' were the enemy.

As important as it is to understand the group pressures that led these ordinary men to join in with the carnage in Józefów, it also needs to be kept in mind that a dozen of the German reservists in Browning's study declined to partake in the massacre. Although this is a very small minority, their actions show that group suggestion does not always sit easily with every individual in all circumstances. In Browning's study, two of the men who refused to take part in the attack explained later that they believed they were freer to decline than some of their comrades because they had no career ambitions within the forces. Others spoke of their objections to the Nazi regime's anti-Semitism (occasionally for political or ideological reasons, and also for practical reasons such as having lost business customers when the anti-Jewish laws had been introduced in Germany). With looser ties to the group for these different reasons, these men identified less closely with the battalion and correspondingly felt less need or pressure to conform with something that they were not wholeheartedly committed to.

By contrast, where an individual has a compelling desire to preserve his identification with the group, he will find ways to override any qualms he may have about joining in with the group's actions. He can do this, for example, by rationalising away his doubts and disavowing the true significance of his actions. This is well illustrated by one of the policemen in Browning's study who went so far as to convince himself that he was in fact *helping* the Jews of Józefów by shooting their children because, he said, the children would not have survived without their mothers who were also being killed.

Misgivings can also be pushed aside through ever-closer identification with the group, which helps the individual feel that he is just one of many, and so his actions somehow 'don't count' as much as they might in other circumstances. As one of the interrogated policemen in Browning's study said, even if he had not taken part in the shooting, the Jews would have been killed anyway, so his participation did not really make any difference one way or the other. As group norms come to replace the wider norms of society, what might in other circumstances be regarded as shameful transgressions come to be seen as acceptable and sometimes even heroic behaviour. In this way, the individual sheds any sense of shame, and his inner eye becomes blinded by a false sense of righteousness.

These processes of suggestibility, conformity and rationalisation have come into play time and again, as individuals have joined in with heinous acts of violent group revenge, from the massacre of Jews in revenge for causing the Black Death in the fourteenth century by purportedly poisoning the water wells of Europe; to the brutal intimidation and violent murder of Black men by white lynch mobs in the American South in the early twentieth century; to the Hutus' grievance-filled slaughter of 800,000 mostly Tutsi men, women and children in Rwanda in 1994. In these, and in so many other tragic cases through history, groups have united around shared grievances and taken revenge against people who were not in fact guilty of causing them any harm.

Groups and Leaders

Freud points out that it is not only the individual's identification with other group members that fosters a "profound alteration in his mental activity", but also the individual's relationship with the group leader. The role of the leader is complex. In his study of group psychology Freud examined leadership in the Church and the Army and found that in both organisations, group members identify with their leader in a way that resembles how they might relate to a father figure. First, there is a narcissistic identification with the leader in the sense that group members unconsciously wish to *be* the father/leader; and, at a more conscious level, they wish to be *like* him. Secondly, there is a strong emotional attachment to the father/leader because he provides a sense of safety and a sense of belonging. This attachment is expressed by group members through their subordination to the will of the leader, or what Sandor Ferenczi called an "impulse to obedience". As both Freud and Ferenczi note, the group's leader can be (like) a primal father: someone who is both feared and loved and who, in exchange for compliance and loyalty, provides followers with a feeling of belonging and a sense of security (Ferenczi 1920, Freud 1921).

A compelling and skilful leader who can cultivate this impulse to obedience will be able to generate support for a programme of radical revenge even where the programme is underpinned by values that group members might *as individuals* have been reluctant to espouse. Through their identification with, and devotion to, the father/leader, group members will find ways to repress or split off their misgivings. Adopting the admired leader's shamelessness as their own, they become champions of the radical revenge that their leader calls for. Just as with group membership, the more the leader's beliefs and wishes correspond to members' (often unconscious) wishes, the greater will be their inclination to follow the leader.

The close identification that can be cultivated between leaders and their followers, and the sinister uses to which this is sometimes put, were eloquently described by the psychoanalyst Roger Money-Kyrle who was invited to attend a Nazi rally shortly before Hitler came to power. Both Goebbels and Hitler addressed the rally and, although they both said more or less the same thing, the audience remained transfixed. What Money-Kyrle observed was that the people attending the rally "seemed gradually to lose their individuality and to become fused into a not very intelligent but immensely powerful monster." It was a monster that was entirely in its creator's thrall. Money-Kyrle describes how during the first part of the rally the audience listened "in an orgy of self-pity" to the speakers bemoaning the suffering of Germany since the Great War. In the second part, these introductory lamentations gave way to an outpouring of vitriol against Jews and Social Democrats who were blamed for all the suffering that the audience had been through. Responding to the segue from grievance to blame, "the monster seemed on the point of becoming homicidal". And then the tone changed once again, as Hitler began to celebrate the growth and power of the Nazi Party, at which point the monster became "intoxicated by the belief in its own omnipotence" (Money-Kyrle 1941, p.166).

Money-Kyrle's vivid account of how Goebbels and Hitler managed to turn a group of individuals into a servile but powerful and seemingly monolithic monster is as remarkable as it is disturbing. In many ways it tallies with what the sociologist Sigmund Neumann described in his study of demagoguery (Neumann 1938). Examining the ways in which a demagogue can secure a devoted following, Neumann found that one of the simplest but most effective tactics available to the demagogue consists in regular and direct communication with his followers. At the time Neumann was writing this would have been primarily through mass meetings and rallies. In the twenty-first century, the demagogue has additionally a range of social media at his disposal through which to communicate directly with his followers. The importance of direct communication lies in its potential for cultivating strong emotional ties with the group, and all the more so when the leader repeatedly uses specific slogans and symbols which then form a common language for the leader and his followers.

Another tactic used by demagogues is what Neumann referred to as the personification of politics. This involves encouraging group members to follow the leader himself rather than adhering to an abstract programme or set of principles. Personification helps to create a sense of the leader as parent, the person who can be counted on to do whatever is necessary to provide protection and prosperity, so long as the group responds with compliance and devotion. Importantly, personification also applies to the demagogue's messages about who is to blame for his followers' suffering. The demagogue will attribute their misery to the evil machinations of specific and identifiable enemies rather than to complex and abstract ideas such as economic trends or technological developments. Identifying a group which can be blamed for his followers' suffering serves two key purposes. Firstly, it underscores the leader's understanding of his followers' grievances; secondly, it provides group members with a target on to which to project their feelings of weakness, humiliation and anger. The group which is blamed will vary from case to case but is usually a relatively weak group that will struggle to defend itself against the projections which beset it. As the dominant group splits off and projects its own anxieties onto the fall guy, the fall guy becomes increasingly identified with anxiety and insecurity, and so is ever-more feared and loathed. The scene is set for radical revenge.

The politics of radical revenge

Unlike dictators who rely on force and terror, leaders in democratic societies depend on the support of the electorate. They garner that support in part through political argument but also by cultivating emotional ties with voters. One of the more cynical ways to develop these ties is by playing into voters' deepest anxieties and their darkest wishes, which often include a wish for radical revenge. This approach, so vividly described by Money-Kyrle, has been adapted and adopted by a number of democratically elected populist leaders in the twenty-first century.

Rodrigo Duterte, who was elected President of the Philippines in 2016, ran his election campaign on a platform known as penal populism. He presented the electorate with a vision of the Philippines as a country consumed by a destructive battle between decent citizens on the one hand, and evil drug traffickers and criminals on the other. Duterte promised to do what previous governments had failed to do, namely to clean up the country so that worthy citizens could once again go about their lives without fear of the unworthy criminal elements of society. His promise served him well, carrying him to the presidency on a wave of popular support.

Using data from over 200 interviews carried out before Duterte's election, Nicole Curato shows that latent anxieties about the country's 'drugs problem' and associated crime already existed in many Philippine communities prior to Duterte's campaign (Curato 2016). Duterte's ability to identify and home in on these anxieties and fears, and his promise to address them if he were elected President, brought him a high level of support from voters who welcomed the promise to take firm measures to clean up their country and return it to the stability that many longed for. These measures offered a form of revenge for the suffering that many voters and their families had endured due to widespread drug trafficking. It is however unlikely that everyone who voted for Duterte anticipated the degree of violence that he would subsequently unleash. Evidence suggests that his 'war on drugs' rapidly escalated into a systematic programme of ruthless killing of the urban poor by a police force empowered to kill anyone suspected of drug use or drug dealing.

In Brazil, Jair Bolsonaro was elected President in 2018 on a law-and-order platform which resonated with groups comprising both the very rich and the very poor who were united in their disaffection and despair over Brazil's rising crime rate and widespread political corruption. Many were captivated by Bolsonaro during his election campaign, in particular by his demonisation of his political enemies and his bold promises to save the country from total ruin (Hunter & Power 2019). Brazil had suffered a severe recession since 2015, with unemployment doubling to over 12%, and GDP shrinking in 2015 and again in 2016. Despite this, Bolsonaro had few economic policies to offer the electorate; instead, he focused on blaming his political opponents and liberals more generally for the country's decline, and promised an end to corruption and a return to the widely longed-for stability. He suggested that criminals should die, leftists should be imprisoned, and that minorities must be stopped from causing Brazil its many social and economic difficulties. These sorts of simplistic promises of radical revenge, rather than a detailed economic programme, won Bolsonaro the support of almost 58 million voters.

One of the most extreme and sustained programmes of radical revenge in recent years was introduced by Donald Trump who in 2016 was elected the 45th President of the United States of America. A Republican demagogue who by 2015 had planted himself firmly on the right wing of his party, he built his election campaign around a nationalist rhetoric encapsulated in his official campaign slogan: "Make America Great Again". This catch-phrase was repeated at campaign rallies, on Twitter and Facebook, and it was emblazoned on his supporters' red baseball hats so that followers could easily recognise and identify with one another wherever they might meet.

Although the slogan Make America Great Again (MAGA) was derided by liberals for what was seen as its shallowness and pretensions, it proved to be extremely effective. MAGA contains an implicit reference to an age gone by, when America was great, life was good, and the social order was as it should be. This idealised picture of the past was central to Trump's appeal to his supporters who wished to regain the privileged status that had at one time accrued to them simply by virtue of being white, or a man; or, most privileged of all, a white man. Conversely, the imagined 'golden age' at the heart of

MAGA held no attraction for Blacks, Hispanics and other minorities who had never enjoyed the status or security of their white counterparts in the US, having instead been persecuted and systematically disadvantaged, generation after generation. For them, there was no great past to return to. Trump's electoral messages played on this split in the US population, and reinforced it rather than trying to heal it.

Trump gained much of his electoral support from older, white, lower middle class and working class men whose traditional way of life and social standing had been eroded by increasing economic insecurity coupled with decades of socially progressive programmes and policies. Globalisation, technological developments, international trade and foul play in the money markets had taken a huge toll on America's lower middle class and working class. A steady increase in cheap foreign imports over the years had led to a decline in domestic industry so that steel mills had closed down, factories packed up, and as many as five million (mostly semi- and unskilled) jobs were lost to foreign competitors. In the fifteen years preceding Trump's election as President, well over 50% of people living in America's metropolitan areas (covering three-quarters of the country's population) had seen their household income decline. The situation worsened considerably for the many people who lost their jobs, their life savings and their homes in the aftermath of the 2008 financial crisis which had been caused by speculators betting ever-higher stakes on the sub-prime mortgage market. For many unskilled and semi-skilled workers and their families, the future looked bleak.

However, this demographic formed only part of Trump's power base. As the economist Paul Krugman observed, "people who were doing well financially were just as likely to support Trump as people who were doing badly". Although this might be an overstatement, Krugman raises a vitally important point, namely that the salient unifying factor among Trump supporters was not so much economic hardship as resentment at "losing status in a changing country, one in which the privilege of being a white man isn't what it used to be." (Krugman 2018). Trump's success was largely due to the way he homed in on this deep sense of loss and gave voice to the latent desire for revenge that it had engendered. Rather than framing the loss as a consequence of decades of global and domestic economic restructuring, Trump personalised it and, in doing this, he helped to convert a demographically heterogeneous group of voters into a relatively cohesive entity that was united by shared grievances and shared (perceived) enemies. The narrative that Trump offered was one which attributed the white man's loss of status and security to the harmful policies of liberal elites represented by President Obama (his Black predecessor in the White House) and Hillary Clinton (his female rival in the presidential election), both of whom he accused in various ways of having let Hispanics, Muslims and other minority groups take away the jobs, prosperity and social status that rightfully belonged to 'true' (i.e. white male) Americans. For Trump – and his followers – it was time for revenge.

President Trump and his programme of radical revenge

During his 2016 election campaign, Trump promised to build a wall along the southern border of the US to prevent what he referred to as "illegal" Mexican immigrants from entering the country, and said he would force Mexico to pay for the wall. He tweeted that Mexican immigrants bring drugs and crime into the US, and that they are rapists. He told Americans, "Mexico is killing us on jobs". He committed himself to deporting at least 11 million undocumented immigrants and to enforcing tighter limits on any future immigration. In a speech given in Phoenix, Arizona in August 2016, Donald Trump said that if he were elected President he would end federal funding to all cities which did not comply with federal immigration policies (these areas, known as 'sanctuary cities', are mainly Democrat strongholds). In January 2017, shortly after he was elected, President Trump called for a total and complete end to any non-US Muslims entering the country, and declared that immigration would be suspended from "places like" Syria and Libya.

In making these sorts of promises and statements Trump stoked up anxieties and instilled paranoia among many American voters who were already feeling socially and economically vulnerable. Like other populists, he lamented an age gone by (when America was "great"), he identified who was to blame for its current social and economic downturn (racial and religious minorities) and he promised his supporters revenge for the injustices they had suffered. The shamelessness with which he singled out minority groups for his enmity brought him ever closer to those voters who had long shared his views but who had previously been more circumspect in expressing them.

Of course Trump did not introduce racism into the US. The country has a long and shameful history of racist violence and hatred stretching back from the days of slavery, through to segregation, to the violence of the Ku Klux Klan and other white supremacist groups, to the horrors of lynching and routine police brutality, through to the many institutional (as well as individual) expressions of racism that continue today.

According to the American Civil Liberties Union (ACLU), although white people engage in drug offences at a higher rate than Black people, Blacks are incarcerated for drug crimes at ten times the rate of whites. Moreover, whereas only 13% of the general population is Black, African Americans make up 42% of people on death row, and 34% of those who have already been executed. Systemic racism is not limited to the justice system. It also shapes the education system, where even at pre-school level (age two to five years), Black pupils are much more likely to be suspended than whites, a trend which continues right the way up the school ladder (US Department of Education Office for Civil Rights 2014). Racism is also embedded in the US political system. The perverse tactics used in Southern states in the late nineteenth and early twentieth centuries to prevent Black Americans from voting helped to disenfranchise large numbers of (mainly Democrat-voting) people for decades. Voters at that time were required to pass literacy tests, or to guess how many jelly beans were in a jar, and it was left up to the white local polling clerks to decide whether prospective voters had passed the test (Sopel 2018). These sorts of practices were eventually deemed undemocratic and unconstitutional. They were duly abolished, only to be replaced by more discreetly racist measures. For example, some polling sites have introduced later opening times and earlier closing times, a practice which disproportionately precludes Black citizens from voting because of their employment patterns. Other measures have included the imposition of impossibly restrictive rules on voter identification, ostensibly as a means of preventing voter fraud, although widely regarded as another means of excluding Black Americans and other minority groups. Alongside these more insidious forms of racism, there has been more overtly racist violence expressed more or less continuously, including the many flagrant cases of police brutality against Black men.

The civil rights movement of the 1960s marked the beginning of sustained efforts to abolish at least some of the more blatant and systematic expressions of racism. Through the introduction and implementation of a range of legislative and educational reforms, racism became less accepted, both legally and socially. Society's norms have very gradually changed and, although racism is still deeply embedded in many parts of the US, there is more shame and disapprobation attached to openly racist views and actions than was the case before the civil rights movement began the fight for social justice.

This slow and unsteady process of reform was dramatically reversed by President Trump[16]. Throughout his campaigning and his Presidency, Trump propounded a Manichean view of the country, in which the 'ordinary' (i.e. white) American was represented as being unfairly under siege by minority groups. Through his words and actions, he told his supporters that it was legitimate to want – and to take – revenge against these minorities and their liberal political representatives.

President Trump was forthright about wishing to reverse many of the policies that had been introduced by his predecessor. President Obama had long been a hated rival, not only because of his liberal values but also because of a personal vendetta rooted in a 2011 incident in which Obama had publicly shamed Trump at the White House Correspondents' Dinner (which itself had been an act of revenge against Trump's 'birther' conspiracy theories). Trump's vengeful attacks on Obama's legacy were perhaps most

---

16 A 2019 survey carried out by the Pew Research Center found that 65% of Americans (across racial and ethnic groups) believed that it had become more common for people to express racist or racially insensitive views since Trump was elected President (Pew Research Center 2019).

explicit in his repeated efforts to undermine the Affordable Care Act, an Act which Obama had been deeply committed to and closely identified with. There were other examples, too. Within months of being elected, for instance, Trump announced that he was going to cancel the Deferred Action on Childhood Arrivals (DACA) which Obama had introduced. Trump's Attorney General, Jeff Sessions, claimed that DACA favoured 'lawbreakers' who would harm the wages and employment of native-born Americans.

What was even more influential than these vengeful policies, however, was the revenge culture that Trump fostered and condoned through his tweets and speeches. In August 2017 he famously suggested that there was a moral equivalence between far-right demonstrators (including a large number of neo-Nazis and white nationalists) and liberal counter-protesters in Charlottesville, Virginia, announcing to the world's media that there had been "some very fine people on both sides". The month after he made this statement, there was a significant spike in reported hate crimes nationally.

Trump's support for violent revenge against liberals and minorities went further than this. In the same year that he had said there were fine people on both sides of the Charlottesville protests, Trump praised the Republican Congressional candidate Greg Gianforte for having body slammed a journalist who had asked him a question he didn't like. Trump was cheered by a crowd of 8,000 supporters when he referred to Gianforte as "my guy". In 2018, the day after staff at CNN and a number of prominent Democrats had been sent packages containing explosive devices, Trump tweeted that much of the anger in the US was the fault of media itself, a barely veiled suggestion that CNN (regarded as a liberal broadcaster) had only itself to blame for the revenge that it had been subjected to.

In making these sorts of statements in his role as President of the United States, Donald Trump legitimised acts of hatred and violence against minorities, and against those who supported them. After a 2015 terrorist shooting in California by a couple which happened to be Muslim, candidate Trump called for a complete ban on Muslims entering the country. Over the next ten days, hate crimes against Muslims and Arabs in the US rose by 23%. When six Baltimore policemen were charged in 2017 with crimes relating to the death of a 25-year-old Black man while in custody, a local lawyer expressed little surprise that this had happened, referencing President Trump's remarks earlier that year in which he urged police not to be "too nice" when transporting suspects. In Boston, two white brothers brutally attacked and urinated on a homeless Latino man. Later, they said that they had targeted their victim because they believed he was an illegal immigrant, and that Donald Trump was right that "all these illegals need to be deported". When Trump heard about the incident his response was to observe that "...people who are following me are very passionate. They love this country and they want this country to be great again." He could not have been clearer in his endorsement of radical revenge.

From 'lock her up' to 'send her back'

In his 2016 bid to become President, Donald Trump faced a formidable opponent in Hillary Clinton. She had been a Senator, a Secretary of State and a prominent First Lady. Donald Trump had been a flamboyant businessman and a reality TV star. But Trump was not cowed by his rival's superior political experience and breadth of knowledge. If he was, he hid it well by belittling and denigrating Clinton at every turn. In doing this he demonstrated his willingness to breach social norms and values in order to reach his goal, a process through which he won the support and even the affection of voters who felt they wanted to be on the same side as this mighty father/leader who promised a better life.

Some of the most vicious attacks on Clinton followed the discovery during the election campaigning season that as Secretary of State she had used her private email server for official business, which led initially to speculation regarding possible corruption. Within a short time, an FBI investigation found that although Clinton had been careless, there was no evidence of any criminal activity. Nevertheless, the Republican Party seized on the issue, and exploited it as an opportunity to discredit and disgrace Clinton. At the Party's National Convention in July 2016, calls rose for Hillary Clinton to be jailed. The New Jersey governor Chris Christie (who had pulled out of the Presidential contest and decided instead to back

Trump's candidacy) asked the crowd repeatedly whether Clinton was 'guilty or not guilty'. Although officially cleared by the FBI of any criminal intent, the crowd understood that the correct answer for Christie was 'guilty'. No thought was given to the details of the case, to the fact that harm had been neither intended nor caused by Clinton's acts. Instead, the crowd took up the suggestion immediately and shouted that Clinton was guilty. Soon the crowd erupted in calls to 'lock her up', much to the delight of Christie and other Republican politicians. Within a short time, 'lock her up' became one of the most popular rallying cries of the Republicans' 2016 election campaign.

The relish with which Trump's followers called for Trump to 'lock her up' highlights how a leader can sway a group and unite it with crude and simple slogans. It also reveals the visceral connection between Trump and his supporters. The evident pleasure with which the crowds called for Clinton to be locked up was matched by Trump's appreciation of their support, expressed though his clapping in time to the chanting, and his beaming smile of approval as the calls for revenge rose up. The crowd's delight in many ways had little to do with the content of what was being chanted; it was about the fact of being able to say it, of being able to express the anger, the bitterness, the envy and the hatred that had been suppressed for so long. Trump had broken with long-established tradition by referring to his fellow presidential candidate provocatively and entirely disrespectfully as 'crooked Hillary'; his supporters took their cue from their leader and called for 'crooked Hillary' to be locked up. And so the connection between Trump and his supporters was strengthened. The clearest indication that the significance of the 'lock her up' chant was affective rather than substantive came within days of Trump being elected, when he made it clear that he in fact had no intention of prosecuting his erstwhile opponent.

Another reason the chant was significant is that it revealed how important revenge was for many of Trump's followers. It would not be enough to win against Clinton at the ballot box, they were calling for more: they wanted Hillary Clinton to be humiliated and punished: not for her emails but for being the representative of the liberal values that had over many years changed the nature of American society to their disadvantage. For this, they wanted revenge – radical revenge which, like the revenge of a lynch mob, took no account of reasonableness, culpability or proportionality. Although the crowd could not secure Clinton's imprisonment, they found other ways to humiliate her, including the use of slogans such as 'Hillary For Prison 2016' accompanied by a series of misogynistic and demeaning images of the Secretary of State.

Three years later, Trump's 2019 campaign for re-election in 2020 revealed once again his ability to express and legitimise the vengeful thoughts and feelings of his supporters, and to harness them in support of his leadership bid[17]. In mid-July 2019 President Trump began something of a crusade against four Democrats in the House of Representatives. All four of these politicians were women of colour, and all four were progressive politicians who had been vocal in calling for a reversal of Trump's anti-immigration policies. President Trump's response to their opposition to his policies was to tweet that the four women should "go back and help fix the totally broken and crime infected places from which they came". The fact that three out of the four Representatives were US-born, and the fourth was a naturalised citizen from the age of 17, seemed irrelevant. What Trump was saying in his tweet was that, as women of colour who opposed him, these four members of the House of Representatives were un-American and they did not belong in the US.

A few days later, the crowd at a campaign rally in Greenville, North Carolina showed the depth of their support for Trump. As he began talking about the four Congresswomen, singling out in particular the Representative who was not US-born, the crowd began chanting, 'Send her back! Send her back!' with the same punchy cadence that 'Lock her up' had at one time been chanted. The hate-filled chanting grew louder and louder, as the crowd became increasingly animated by their own calls for revenge.

There was considerable political fall-out after the Greenville rally. Consternation was expressed in the national and international mass media at the levels of hatred, anger, vengeance and racism that were so

---

17 At the time of writing, the result of the 2020 Presidential election is as yet unknown.

shamelessly displayed in Greenville. Some of Trump's advisers were moved to suggest in no uncertain terms that Trump should avoid being seen to encourage these chants at future rallies. Perhaps motivated by opinion polls, Trump apparently accepted his advisers' suggestions, and refrained from whipping up calls to 'send her back' at later rallies.

A first-hand account of a Trump re-election rally

In order to get a better feel for the dynamic between President Trump and his followers, I decided to attend a Trump re-election rally. I signed up for the rally which was held on 15th August 2019 in Manchester, New Hampshire, just a few weeks after the Greenville rally. New Hampshire is a relatively small New England state in the northeast of the US, which in the 2016 election was narrowly won by Hillary Clinton. Licence plates on New Hampshire cars bear the state's motto, 'Live Free or Die', a libertarian sentiment embodied in the state's policy of raising neither sales tax nor income tax so that residents remain free to choose how they spend their money. Any public services that the state provides are funded mainly by property tax.

The President's rally was scheduled to begin at 7pm, with Trump delivering his address at 8pm. I thought it would be good to get there early but when I joined the queue of ticket holders at 10am, I saw that I wasn't early at all, as there were already thousands of people queueing up, eagerly waiting for the arena doors to open. The vast majority were white, and most looked over 40 years old, although there were also significant pockets of younger people scattered throughout the crowd. I was surprised to see only slightly more men than women in the queue. Many of the men and women wore red MAGA hats and T-shirts, while others opted for the new slogan for Trump's 2020 re-election campaign which was 'Keep America Great'. A number of people held handmade placards and signs, with slogans that included Gays for Trump, Build the Wall, Keep America Great, Bearing Arms is not a Crime, Trump 2020, and even one which read Thank You Sweet Baby Jesus for My Hot President. Many women held pre-printed signs and wore badges declaring 'Women for Trump'. Overall, there was a festive, almost carnival-like atmosphere among the crowd of supporters, with live music playing throughout the day, and people sharing food and drink, and chatting amicably with one another.

During the course of the day my neighbour in the queue held my place as I intermittently left to speak with other people who were waiting for the rally to begin. I explained to each of them I was doing research for a book and asked if they would be willing to talk with me about their support for Trump. Almost everyone I approached was courteous and willing to share their political views with me. My conversations with them were not intended to generate systematic data, but rather to improve my understanding of what these supporters thought of Trump, what he represented for them, and what role radical revenge might play in all this.

The first people I spoke with were two white middle-aged women who had travelled from Rhode Island to attend the rally. Dressed in sparkly stars-and-stripes T-shirts, they held placards proclaiming their support for the President. The more forthcoming of the two told me that her main reason for supporting Trump was that, unlike previous Presidents, he "talks like us". She had previously voted Democrat but when Trump came on the scene, she knew she wanted to support him because she felt she could relate to him. Her friend agreed, saying that "he just says it like it is". These expressions of close identification with the President were repeated by many of the people I spoke with. There was a feeling that Trump was somehow just like them, and that he understood them in a way that most politicians did not.

One woman told me that she had lost a lot of friends when she became a Trump supporter. She spoke bitterly of how she had been derided on Facebook by former friends because of her political views. I had the strong impression that she had been quite hurt and humiliated by this experience, and I wondered whether her way of managing the painful feelings was to identify all the more closely with Trump the father/leader, as she told me about the many other Trump rallies she had attended. She enjoyed the rallies, she said, because she didn't come up against the nastiness that she'd experienced from her erstwhile Facebook friends. She felt at home here with other Trump supporters.

Other people at the rally spoke similarly about how good it felt to be among fellow Trump supporters, where there was no risk of being laughed at, attacked, or criticised for their views. Being with like-minded people emboldened them, and they felt able to speak more openly. Some identified themselves, either in conversation or on their placards, as part of the 'silent majority' which, thanks to Trump, no longer had to remain silent. It seemed there was strength (and anonymity) to be had from being part of a 'majority', and – safe in the company of other Trump supporters – there was less cause to feel any shame or fear about their political views.

Alongside the strong emotional ties between the rally attendees and their leader was a shared sense of anger at those whom they believed had caused so much damage to their country and to their livelihoods. The enemy ranged from President Obama who had been 'soft' on immigration, to the immigrants themselves. One man wearing a T-shirt that proclaimed '*Trump 2020 – Fuck Your Feelings*' explained that this slogan was a reference to "all the cry-baby Democrats who complain about all the great stuff that Trump has done". He was not the only one to tell me that President Obama had introduced "a bunch of policies that didn't help people like me", and that it was time the country had a President who knew what had to be done and was not afraid of doing it.

Another man I spoke with had travelled from the neighbouring state of Massachusetts to give his support to the President. In his forties, and a father of two, he runs a small business that had suffered, he said, because of the influx of cheap, illegal labour from Mexico. He said he agreed with Trump's commitment to building a wall between the US and Mexico, not because he had anything against Mexicans, but because he did not think it was fair for them to come illegally into the country. I had the strong sense that he genuinely did not think of himself or Trump as racist, and would have challenged anyone who said otherwise. Yet his support for the Trump campaign which had singled out Mexicans as drug users, rapists and criminals who are "killing us on jobs" would suggest otherwise. With regard to Trump, he told me:

> The reason I'm for Trump is that in America we're a country that punches back. You hit us, we hit you back. And for eight years, under Obama, we had the soft, mushy 'I feel sorry for you, you feel sorry for me' sort of thing. Now **we have a guy here who punches back**. And why does he punch back? He punches back for the people, for jobs, for bringing up the economy, making it a lot easier for the middle class to enjoy life a little bit more. We're not rich, but we're sure as hell not poor because we have enough strength in us, and that's what Trump did. **And now we're punching back**.

This seemed an eloquent expression of loyalty to a strong father/leader whom this voter respected, feared and loved for being able to 'punch back' at people who were seen as enemies. It made him feel safe and secure knowing that he had a President/father who was strong and brave enough to take revenge on his behalf.

Others spoke along similar lines, explaining to me their belief that the US had to protect itself from what they felt were too many Mexicans coming into the country and taking jobs. In the same breath – and without any prompting from me – they told me there was nothing racist about their views and that it was nothing to do with the colour of people's skin.

As one man put it, "All these accusations of racism are so wrong. It could be someone my colour, but if they're from Mexico and coming illegally, we don't want them here. They just happen to be brown." This brought to mind Freud's essay on negation in which Freud suggested that when a patient describes a dream and finishes the description by stating, without any prompting, that the dream was definitely not about their mother, the dream was likely to have been about their mother (Freud 1924). Many people I spoke with expressed racist views and then immediately told me they were not racists. This may have reflected a degree of lingering shame at aligning themselves with a flagrantly racist leader; and yet through negation they could allow themselves to continue fervently supporting Trump and his hate-filled policies and racist ideas.

One man told me that he was fed up with being called a racist, and said with anger, "when a white cop shoots a Black kid, he's called a racist, but what happens if a Black cop kills a white kid? Nobody ever calls that racist, do they?" The lack of insight into the structural racism that underlies police brutality against Black men was astonishing, but it also reflected the President's simplistic messages which included, for example, the notion that there were very fine people on both sides of the Charlottesville conflict.

As well as holding out a promise of a better life and a commitment to radical revenge, Trump offered his supporters a highly valued sense of belonging, and a feeling that by being on his side they were on the side not only of justice, but also of strength and security. This was brought home to me when I spoke with a husband and wife who had travelled from Connecticut to attend the rally. They both talked animatedly about the security that they believed Trump had provided them with. The husband said that jobs were much safer now, thanks to President Trump. I mentioned that I had heard on the news that very morning that the US economy could be facing a severe recession and I wondered if this worried them. The husband pushed my comment aside, telling me the President had been absolutely right to give tax breaks to the rich, "because it's the rich who create jobs, so of course they need tax breaks if we want them to create more jobs for us". When I spoke with his wife, I asked about the 'Women for Trump' badge she was wearing and why she thought Trump was good for women. She explained that she supported Trump because of the security he provides for her and her family which was what mattered most to her. At the end of our conversation in which they both heaped praise on Trump, I thanked them and said it seemed they greatly liked their President both as a person and as a politician. To my surprise, they both laughed when I said this and looked knowingly at each other. The wife then told me that, although she supported Trump 100% as her President, she would never let her daughter anywhere near him.

A lone protester

Occasionally one or two protesters walked down the road carrying anti-Trump placards, staying at a respectful distance from the queueing Trump supporters. These were the only moments when the tone changed from a relaxed and jaunty atmosphere to something darker. On one occasion one protester appeared with a sign proclaiming that President Trump is a racist, and members of the crowd responded with anger and vengeance, screaming "Build the Wall! Build the Wall!" louder and louder, until the protester disappeared from sight.

At 4pm the arena doors opened. The first 11,000 people in the queue were allowed in and the rest of the crowd had to settle for watching the rally on a giant outdoor screen. Once inside the massive hall, people bought themselves snacks and chatted with one another. The hall was filled with the sort of rising excitement that normally accompanies a major sporting event. Music blasted at high volume from speakers across the arena, and slowly the seats began to fill up. After a few introductory speakers who spoke mainly about local issues, it was the moment that the crowd had been waiting for. Bright lights of red, white and blue swept the room and the stage. Thunderous chants of "USA! USA! USA!" and "Four more years! Four more years! Four more years!" accompanied President Trump as he walked onto the stage, turning in different directions to clap his appreciation for his audience, smiling broadly and approvingly at the support they were showing for him. The chanting and clapping continued for some five minutes before Trump began to address his followers.

During his address, whenever Trump mentioned his potential rivals in the 2020 election, the crowd responded immediately with derisory laughter and roars of 'Boo-oo-oo'. Trump stopped speaking intermittently to give the group a space to proclaim its hatred for their shared enemies. Then Trump shifted attention to his own campaign and asked the crowd how they felt about the slogan 'Make America Great Again'. The response was a deafening roar of approval. The notes I wrote straight after the rally included the following:

An invisible link between T [Trump] and crowd – he could switch them from 'yay' to 'boo' with just a sentence and then back again from boo to yay. He said MAGA was honestly the best slogan in history, do you agree – and they agreed and clapped and shouted yay. But then he said, do we give up MAGA? Because we're there already. So maybe the time has come for 'Keep America Great' and the crowd goes wild. He asks them – do we give up MAGA? for Keep America Great? Who's in favour of Keep America Great? And there's a huge and long "Yay! USA!" Surprisingly little content to his speech – but a great deal of connection. He seems to know how to build the connection without content.

What struck me, in other words, was the group's suggestibility, particularly when in the presence of the father/leader whom they loved and respected because of the strength and security he promised them. Trump was adept at fostering these feelings. At the New Hampshire rally he asked the crowd what their views were on the new slogan and in doing this the President shrewdly enhanced his followers' belief that they were an important part of a movement which Trump was the head of. It gave them a feeling of belonging and of being appreciated: the crowd felt they were no longer the powerless, silent majority.

Trump was more than the loving father. He was also the father who demanded loyalty. Turning to economic matters, he told his supporters that the financial markets would have crashed in 2016 if he had not become President, and that the crash could still happen if he weren't re-elected in 2020. Trump told his followers: "You have no choice but to vote for me, because your 401(k)'s down the tubes, everything's going be down the tubes. So whether you love me or hate me, you gotta vote for me."[18]

In New Hampshire there were a few half-hearted attempts to start up the Greenville chants of 'send her back', but they failed to gain ground. A few more voices joined in calls to 'lock her up' when Trump referred to Hillary Clinton, but these calls were similarly short-lived. Trump did not encourage the chanting in the way that he had a few weeks earlier in Greenville. This was almost certainly because of the fallout after Greenville, and the advice

---

18 401(k) refers to US workplace-based pension savings plans.

from his officials that these sorts of calls for revenge were, for the time being at least, counter-productive. The restraint, in other words, was the result of a political decision by the leader, and the crowd deferred.

What was most striking about the rally was the intensity of the bond between the supporters themselves, and between supporters and their President. Trump had promised to take revenge against those who were accused of having caused deep economic difficulties and social discord. He had gone some way to delivering on this revenge by introducing anti-immigration policies that focussed on Hispanics and Muslims, and by making racist statements that shamelessly condoned racist practices and radical revenge. For this, his supporters gave him their thanks and their support. Sitting in the New Hampshire arena, it seemed to me that if the President had called for ever more militant forms of radical revenge against those who were blamed for the group's grievances, he would likely have secured the support of many who were there in the room with him.

Chapter Five
Radically Different Revenge

In *The Better Angels of Our Nature*, Steven Pinker refers to revenge as one of our "inner demons". The urge for revenge is understandable, he says, in so far as it aims for deterrence and what he calls "just desserts". But he goes on to argue that revenge, and the violence which it generates, would be better replaced by cooperation and empathy – namely, the better angels of our nature. Pinker is not alone in taking this view. Social psychologists, game theorists, and many of the world's religious, spiritual, and community leaders have advocated a similar message. Mostly however this has been to no avail. Revenge remains as pervasive as ever, and stubbornly refuses to give way to forgiveness or cooperation (Pinker 2011; Axelrod 1984; McCullough 2008).

This chapter takes a somewhat different approach. Rather than seeing revenge as inherently demonic and by definition destructive, it considers whether revenge can be a force for creativity. There is, for instance, the powerful argument put forward by Aristotle (and discussed later in this chapter) that giving up the desire for revenge in the face of injustice is nothing better than being a slave. There are also emotional and psychological issues to be considered before dismissing revenge as an unmitigated evil. If after being treated unfairly we struggle against any urge for revenge, we may experience feelings of resentment and anger which can fester and eventually become toxic. It can lead to what appears outwardly to be resigned acceptance or forgiveness, but is in fact an inner (sometimes unconscious) harbouring of grievance and bitterness (Steiner 1996). This can eventually come to be expressed in other destructive, and often self-destructive, ways.

The premise of this book is that revenge *per se* is neither angel nor demon. The urge for revenge is a fact of life and what matters most is *whether and how* this urge is enacted. The cases examined in Chapters

Two and Three were cases of radical revenge that were shaped by the individuals' specific pathologies. Revenge for them had to be radical because the individuals were unable to distinguish between the immediate cause of a particular grievance on the hand and, on the other hand, the shame and pain associated with earlier experiences which had made subsequent experiences of shame or envy feel so unbearable and unforgivable. Often under the spell of delusional thinking, the individuals concerned felt compelled to take radical revenge against people who were not guilty in reality of having caused any grievance at all.

Fortunately, not everyone who desires revenge needs *radical* revenge. In most cases, the urge to pay someone back for a harm can be satisfied through a gratifying fantasy, or through ordinary acts of revenge. Often a quick shove, the hoot of a car horn, or a snide remark will suffice. In other cases, revenge can be taken through the law courts which mete out retributive justice. But what happens if ordinary revenge is not enough, and retributive justice is either inappropriate, inadequate, or unavailable? Are there any alternatives to the destructiveness of radical revenge? This chapter tells the stories of four remarkable people who suffered terrible harms at the hands of their aggressors, and describes how they each found creative and life-affirming ways to take revenge without destroying the lives of others.

Is revenge even possible in the face of radical evil?

Can revenge have any meaning at all in the context of an evil that is so vast, so heinous, and so extreme as to be, quite literally, beyond most of our imaginations? This was how Hannah Arendt conceived of the radical evil that for her was embodied by totalitarianism and which, taken to its logical conclusion, resulted in the concentration camps of Nazi Germany. Having first been stripped of their civil rights by the Nazi regime, Jews and other minorities were eventually forced into concentration camps where they endured such devastating physical deprivation and psychological horror that many eventually lost their capacity for solidarity with others and their sense of common humanity. This, argued Arendt, was the desired result of the Nazi totalitarian regime which had used concentration camps in order to dehumanise the inmates and ultimately render them utterly superfluous (Arendt 1951).

The steps the Nazis took in order to achieve their goal are well-known, and hardly need detailed description here. Victims were torn away from their families and communities in order to be transported like animals in hideously overloaded trains to the camps; they were forced to watch as their loved ones were selected for immediate death in gas chambers; they were stripped of their clothing and belongings, sometimes even the hair on their heads, and made to wear threadbare prison uniforms; and they lived and laboured in filthy and over-crowded conditions, being given just enough food to keep (some of) them alive. In addition to all this, as Arendt notes, there was a raft of further measures to reduce the inmates' will to live, including a random and sadistic system of brutal punishments that had no connection with crimes actually committed; and the introduction of a hierarchy within the inmate population so that some inmates were forced to make impossible choices, such as between the murder of their friend or the murder of their family. It was a system that led to despair, hopelessness, spiritual numbness and eventually physical death for millions of inmates.

A personal note

Is any sort of revenge possible against a system of such intricate and profound evil? This question has undoubtedly been lurking somewhere in the back of my mind for most of my life, as both of my parents were Polish Jews and survivors of Nazi concentration camps. Neither of them spoke a great deal about their experiences but over the years they told my sisters and me enough for us to know something of what they went through, and for us to be able to imagine how they had managed to survive.

My mother, who was 15 years old when the war broke out, came from a close-knit orthodox family in a small village in southern Poland. Not long after the Nazis occupied the country, her father thought the family would be safer if they moved to a town with a larger Jewish population, and so the family relocated to nearby Będzin. My maternal grandfather's plan was only partially successful, as my mother and my aunt were eventually selected by the Bedzin town elders to be among those who were transported to concentration camps. Their parents and three brothers survived the war mostly by hiding in primitive garden huts and dark cellars, at the mercy of those who were willing to shelter them, some in exchange for money and others out of a sense of moral duty towards a fellow human being. Throughout her years in different camps, working under hideously harsh conditions and struggling to survive against all the odds, my mother held on firmly to the hope that the rest of her family were still safe and alive.

My father was 18 when the war began. He had been born and raised in Będzin where he lived with his mother, father, older sister and younger brother. He attended the Jewish school there and by all accounts was a gifted pupil who excelled in history and philosophy. His bright future was stolen from him in 1942, when he was the first member of his family to be transported, initially to Ottmuth forced labour camp where he was put to work building highways. From Ottmuth he was moved to Markstadt (another forced labour camp) and from Markstadt to a string of different concentration camps. Living and working in dire conditions, he eventually contracted tuberculosis which weakened him severely. Towards the end of the war, as the Nazis fled the Allied forces, my father was forced to join a death march which he barely survived.

Undoubtedly what helped my father stay alive through all this terror and hardship was having fallen in love with the woman who was later to become his wife and my mother. They had met briefly before the war in Bedzin, but it was during the war, when their paths crossed at Markstadt, that they fell in love. My father once told me that my mother had saved his life on at least three different occasions, including the time she risked her own life in order to bring him potatoes to nourish him while he was recovering from TB (she was working in the Markstadt kitchen at the time). I imagine that she also saved his life by giving him hope in an otherwise hopeless world.

After the war my mother's deepest wish came true as she was reunited with her family all of whom had, quite miraculously, survived. A short time later, she and her family moved to Munich as displaced persons. My father suffered further trauma however, when he received the news that his mother, his father, his beloved younger brother, his uncles, aunts and most of his cousins had all been murdered, many of them in Auschwitz which is just 50 kilometres south of Bedzin.

Meanwhile, as soon as she was able to, my mother searched the list of survivors compiled by the International Red Cross to find out what had happened to the man she had fallen so deeply in love with. Overjoyed to find that he was alive, she managed to track him down and – to cut a long story short – they were reunited, married, and in 1951 they left Munich for the US where they hoped to build a new life.

Many people are shocked to hear that, after suffering so deeply at the hands of the Nazi regime, Jewish people would choose to live in Munich of all places! Munich was known to be Hitler's favourite city. It was here that he made his failed putsch in 1923. It was a city that had become closely associated with Hitler's eventual rise to power, and with Nazism more generally. I once asked my father how on earth they could have gone to live in Munich so soon after the war. He told me that for him – and for many other Jewish concentration camp survivors – being in Germany shortly after the war was a way of saying: "We survived. You tried to kill us off, you tried to get rid of us, but you didn't. We're here, and we're alive." And this assertion of *being*, in the face of the Nazis' efforts to turn them into *not-being*, seems to me to contain the beginning of an answer to the question of what revenge can look like in the context of truly radical evil.

Physical and Metaphysical Revenge

In a thought-provoking paper on holocaust literature as a form of revenge, Lily Halpert-Zamir suggests that revenge is fundamentally rooted in our "archaic instinct for justice" (Halpert-Zamir 2018). Paraphrasing Aristotle, she writes that if a person "contents himself with injustice, it is not only his body that is defeated but also his spirit", with the result that he is no better than a slave. By contrast, an urge for revenge in the face of injustice signifies that the would-be avenger remains in possession of his dignity and autonomy, and that he therefore has a capacity for moral freedom. Seen in this light, the desire to take revenge when an injustice has been done can be understood as life-affirming and a source of moral status.

But how can one avenge an injustice that is so profound and so egregious that it is almost impossible to put into words? Perhaps the best way to address this question is by drawing on the distinction highlighted by Halpert-Zamir between physical revenge on the one hand, and metaphysical revenge on the other, and by noting the inadequacy of physical revenge in the face of extreme harm and injustice. Drawing on Nietzsche, Halpert-Zamir describes physical revenge as a more or less immediate and concrete response to a harm suffered, a response that is made under the pressure of time so as to be effected before the memory of the harm fades and becomes a thing of the past. The point here is that once a harm has become part of the fading past, it can no longer be changed and so it remains embedded in the victim's being. Physical revenge is in essence an attempt to make good a harm in an immediate and concrete way by inflicting a comparable harm on the aggressor.

Conversely, metaphysical revenge (in the sense of being beyond just physical) is not constrained by time. On the contrary, the revenge-seeker is, if anything, strengthened by the passing of time which enables him to gather resolve and clarity. What is of critical importance is that, over time, the injustice which has been suffered does not poison the person's mind or spirit (as it did, for example, in the cases of Mark Barton and Shawn Sayer). Instead, the injustice becomes a source of resolve and vitality, and the suffering which was once experienced is transformed into a sense of independence from, and superiority over, the aggressor through the creation of something valued that is beyond the reaches of the aggressor.

Different responses to the Nazi genocide provide a neat illustration of this distinction between physical and metaphysical revenge. After the war, many felt that the justice meted out at the Nuremburg trials had been a wholly inadequate response to the Nazis' crimes against humanity. With the Shoah still fresh in their minds, a group of Jewish men formed a clandestine group known as Nokmim (Hebrew for 'Avengers') comprising around 50 members and led by the writer Abba Kovner and his associates. Their aim was to take physical revenge on behalf of the six million Jews who had died at the hands of the Nazis. Their guiding principle was talion: an eye for an eye, a tooth for a tooth. Nokmim's strategy was to poison the water supplies in four major German cities in order to kill six million Germans. Although strictly speaking this was proportionate, it was to be radical revenge which would take no account of culpability or intentionality in so far as the victims of the plan would have included German men, women and children who had not necessarily caused or even supported the deaths of the six million Jews.

In the event, the plan to poison the water supplies was scuppered and Abba Kovner was arrested and imprisoned. Many of his co-conspirators remained committed to vengeance however and, led by 21-year old Joseph Harmatz, the group reverted to a Plan B, which was to poison more than 10,000 German prisoners of war (POWs) who were being held in a camp near Nuremburg. On 20 April 1946 the New York Times reported that 1,900 German POWs at the US run POW camp had become seriously ill after having eaten bread laced with arsenic. Three days later, the total number of POWs affected by the poison had reached 2,283. Many of them became seriously ill, but no fatalities were ever confirmed. Initially the poisoning of the bread was attributed to accidental contamination with a chemical used for killing cockroaches but by 23 April the New York Times reported evidence of a "mysterious plot against 15,000 former Nazi Elite Guard men" who had been confined in the camp near Nuremberg.

When Joseph Harmatz died at the age of 91, his obituary noted that he never publicly expressed any regret for his involvement in either of the plans to take revenge for the suffering that he, his family, and six million other Jews had been through. His only regret, his son said, was that the second attempt at revenge (Plan B) did not work out as well as he had hoped, namely with the deaths of thousands of Nazi POWs. Joseph Harmatz had lost almost all of his family to Nazi persecution, and for this – and the deaths of millions of other Jews – he never stopped wanting revenge. It is difficult to know, however, how many deaths would have been enough. Would 11,000 deaths have sufficed? Or 15,000? Or would six million German deaths have sufficed? And sufficed for what?

The British journalist Jonathan Freedland has written about Nokmim's efforts to take revenge in the context of the Allies' post-war efforts to bring to justice tens of thousands of men and women who were part of the vast Nazi machine (Freedland 2008). This was a case of retributive justice feeling so paltry, so utterly deficient, that those who were directly affected felt impelled towards physical revenge. Freedland writes that of the 13.2 million Germans in post-war West Germany who were regarded in one way or another as having been part of the Nazi apparatus, fewer than 3.5 million were charged and, of these, 2.5 million were released without trial. Of the remaining million, most suffered nothing more than a fine or the confiscation of some property, or in some cases a temporary restriction on their future employment. By 1949, from the original list of 13 million perpetrators, just 300 were in prison. It was against this background, Freedland suggests, that Harmatz and the members of Nokmim were driven to take radical physical revenge, partly to prevent the memory of the Nazi horrors from becoming part of a fading past.

Although it is easy to understand the gratification that would derive from a *fantasy* of making the numbers of lost lives more or less equivalent on both sides, it is more difficult to imagine that actually killing six million Germans would have made good, or even alleviated, the suffering of those who had lost their health and well-being, as well as their love ones, to the Shoah. It would have been a physical revenge that might have brought temporary gratification but which would not, and could not, have made good the horrors of the past.

Four remarkable stories of revenge

(i) A path to metaphysical revenge: Martin Greenfield's story

The metaphysical revenge taken by many holocaust survivors was much less concrete and talionic than Nokmim's efforts at revenge. It was a quietly powerful statement of defiance in the face of Nazi efforts to make their victims redundant, inhuman and superfluous, as Martin Greenfield's story shows. Martin is a Jewish man, now in his nineties, who lives in Brooklyn, New York, where over many years he has built a thriving business as a master tailor specialising in men's suits. He was born in 1928 in what was then Czechoslovakia. In April 1944 – on the second day of Passover – he and many other Jews from his village were transported to a camp in Hungary where he watched a Gestapo guard force his grandfather to the ground before cutting off the elderly man's long beard. From there Martin and much of his family were transported to Auschwitz where his mother, sisters, brother and grandparents were all immediately put to death. Martin and his father were the only members of the family to survive these early 'selections'. Shortly afterwards, Martin was shocked when his father explained to him that the two of them could not stay together, that they would have to separate and each fend for themselves. With time, Martin realised that his father did not want his son to risk his own life by helping his older and weaker father. In his memoir, Greenfield tells us that his father told him, "On your own, you will survive. You are young and strong, and I know you will survive. If you survive by yourself, you must honor us by living, by not feeling sorry for us. That is what you must do." To this day, Martin remains grateful to his father for those words which helped him replace 'survivor guilt' with a sense of purpose, and a reason to go on living (Greenfield 2014).

In February 1945, having survived deprivation, terrible loss and cruelty, Martin was transported to the Buchenwald concentration camp where he was put to work in the munitions factory. One day he was ordered to join a small team of prisoners who had been instructed to carry out some repairs outside of the camp in the nearby city of Weimar. Martin was glad for the opportunity to leave the camp, to be able to see the sky and get away from the stench of rotting corpses. And, he thought, there might also be a possibility of finding a potato as they trudged across the fields to get to Weimar.

Martin and his fellow-inmates were set to work repairing the mansion of the Mayor of Weimar. While he was there he noticed two rabbits in a cage which contained the remains of the rabbits' dinner. Martin took the wilted lettuce leaf and the half-eaten carrot out of the cage and hungrily began to eat, but he stopped when he heard a voice yelling at him, asking what he was doing. It was the mayor's wife, holding a baby in her arms. She was enraged to see this 'animal' stealing her rabbits' food and she immediately reported him to the nearby SS officer who set about bludgeoning Martin's back with his baton. Martin returned to Buchenwald in terrible pain. Looking back to that time, he writes: "In that moment my numbness to death melted. In its place rose an alien bloodlust, a hunger for vengeance unlike any I had ever known. The surge of adrenaline and rush of rage felt good inside my withered frame. Then and there I made a vow to myself: if I survived Buchenwald, I would return and kill the mayor's wife." (Greenfield 2014, p.49)

In writing this, Martin illustrates the Aristotelian view of the desire for revenge as being life-affirming: what had previously been his 'numbness to death' was replaced by an energy that was fired by a desire for revenge. It warmed up his cold body and kept him going through the next few weeks. Then, on 11 April 1945, American troops liberated the inmates of Buchenwald. Martin was elated by the thought of freedom, but he could not rid himself of tormenting thoughts about the mayor's wife. Still racked with rage and a lust for revenge, Martin decided he had to keep the promise that he had made to himself, which was to return to Weimar in order to kill her. Accompanied by two young Jewish men, and armed with guns taken from the now abandoned SS supply of weapons, he set off for Weimar.

As he approached the mayor's house, Martin was overwhelmed both by anger and by anguish, not only because of the memory of the mayor's wife's cruelty, but also because of thoughts about all that he had lost, all that he had been through, and all that he had witnessed over the previous six years. He knew that killing the mayor's wife would not – could not – pay the Nazis back for all their ruthless depravity but, Martin told himself, at least it would be a start. As he entered the house, he saw the mayor's wife, once again holding a baby in her arms. Seeing his gun, she begged him not to shoot. He reminded her who he was, and what she had done to him. He then told her he was going to kill her. And yet... on hearing her pleas and hearing the baby cry, Martin wavered. His two companions urged him on, reminding him of all the Jewish babies that the Nazis had killed, but Martin realised that he could not pull the trigger. He could not kill this woman who had called him an animal and who had had him beaten for eating her rabbit's lettuce leaf. Looking back to that moment, Martin said, "That was the moment I became human again". In that moment, Martin regained his sense of self. He realised that physical revenge, taking an eye for an eye, would not restore his losses. Instead, it would have shamed him, particularly in view of the promise that he had made to his father. He realised that taking revenge for the horrors of the holocaust would be far more complex than simply killing the woman standing in front of him.

Each and every person who went through the horrors of the Nazi concentration camps had their own experience of trauma and responded to it in his or her own way. Many suffered from lifelong depression and struggled to rebuild their lives; for many, the regrets, grief, guilt and terrible sense of loss were too much to bear. For those who were fortunate to have the necessary internal resources, a healthy physical constitution and a large amount of good luck, it was possible to carry on living defiantly, proudly and justly. With his father's words always at the back of his mind, Martin Greenfield was able to defy the Nazis' aim to make him superfluous. After the war he went on to have a family and to build a successful career as a New York tailor. In honouring his father's injunction and rebuilding his life, he felt he was taking sweet revenge. It was a metaphysical revenge through which Martin achieved an independence from, and superiority over, his aggressors. He liked to think that he had taken his revenge not just for himself, but also on behalf of his whole family and the six million other Jews who had perished.

(ii) Reforming retributive justice: Carrie Goldberg's story

Shoah survivors like Martin Greenfield are of course not alone in finding creative ways to take revenge. Another example of a radically different and life-affirming approach to revenge is provided by Carrie Goldberg. Having suffered severe abuse both in person and online, she initially sought justice through the legal system. Confronted by the inadequacies of existing laws in punishing perpetrators of revenge porn and other cybercrimes, Carrie realised she would need to find some other way of getting revenge. In her tireless campaigning for legal reform on behalf of other victims of online abuse, she has found a way to satisfy her own need for revenge.

Carrie Goldberg is a Brooklyn-based lawyer in her early 40s. She grew up in Washington State in the northwest corner of the United States, studied English at Vassar College, and then moved to New York City where, after training as a lawyer, she began working for a charity advocating for elderly and mentally incapacitated people. Around this time Carrie began online dating and, after a few unsuccessful meetings, she met a man through the dating website OKCupid who sounded interesting. He said he was a doctor and, from her exchange of messages with him, Carrie thought he seemed intelligent and engaging. On meeting him in person she quickly decided otherwise, but she did not have the opportunity to tell him that she was not interested in pursuing a relationship with him. Instead, she unwittingly drank the beverage he had spiked, and later only had a hazy memory of the violent, perverse and brutal things he did to her, some of which she describes in her book, *Nobody's Victim: Fighting Psychos, Stalkers, Pervs and Trolls*. Later, her memories were confirmed as he had evidently taken photographs while attacking and raping her, and he had begun to post the photographs online (Goldberg 2019).

The trauma was overwhelming. Carrie felt unable to report it to the police because she feared having to undergo intrusive tests to confirm the rape and having to repeat time and again what she could barely bring herself to talk about. She thought of taking legal action against her assailant, but could not countenance the exposure and pain that this would entail. Meanwhile, she was living with the effects of the trauma which, she said, kept her awake at night and made her want to sleep all day.

Months later, in what she later understood to have been an attempt to return to normality, she went back online, hoping to find someone who would help her feel safe and secure. She met a man who appeared to fit the bill: he seemed clever, attentive and physically strong. Carrie was charmed by him, and began to drop her defences. She told him many of her private thoughts and secrets, and let him know about the abuse that she had suffered under the influence of a spiked drink. Within a short time, what had seemed clever turned into manipulative, and what had felt attentive became jealous, possessive and controlling. After much heartache, Carrie left the man who had initially seemed like 'Mr Right'. This marked the beginning of his open campaign of terror, in which he bombarded Carrie with texts and phone messages, and threatened to reveal her secrets to others. Worst of all, he let her know that he had secretly video recorded their sexual activities and was going to send naked still photographs of her to her family, friends and colleagues, as well as to the judges to whom she addressed herself in her daily work as a lawyer.

Carrie's efforts to use the justice system to prevent this man from carrying out his threats proved frustrating and ultimately futile. She spoke with police officers, lawyers and judges only to find out that he was legally entitled to use these naked pictures of her, even though he had taken them without her consent and wanted to use them without her consent. What emerged was that the man who was threatening to subject Carrie to further harm by exposing and shaming her, was protected by the First Amendment of the US Constitution which guarantees freedom of speech and expression.

The combined impact of being threatened and abused by her ex, and then finding that the law offered her no protection, was profound. Carrie felt defeated and, at one point, suicidal. She later attributed her suicidal thoughts to her profound hopelessness at that stage in her life, a time when the idea of death felt like a comfort, and a solution to her pain. There may also have been a revenge component in her thoughts about suicide, a conscious or unconscious desire to punish the men who had hurt her. Yet, at the same time, somewhere in her mind there was an awareness that death would not only end her pain, but it would also end her life; and an awareness too that her death would be neither a fitting nor an effective punishment for the perpetrators of her suffering. Her determination to live proved stronger than the feelings of hopelessness that had temporarily overwhelmed her. And so Carrie set about re-building her life, focussing her energies on what she calls "the transformative power of fighting back". As a trained lawyer, fighting back meant working painstakingly within the legal system. As a woman who had suffered terrible abuse and a violation of her privacy, fighting back meant finding a way to punish her abusers even if this required getting changes to existing laws where they failed to address grievances such as her own.

In the years that followed her sexual abuse and trauma, Carrie set up her own law firm specialising in the rights of victims of sexual assault, stalking and blackmail. Her clients have had their sexual privacy invaded; many have lost friends, money, homes, jobs and places at school as a result of the abuse they have suffered. As she describes it, Carrie fights for her clients like a "ruthless motherfucker", securing wherever possible financial compensation and restraining orders, while also seeking to expose and ensure the imprisonment of offenders. She is, in other words, the sort of lawyer she would have wanted when she was the victim of on- and offline abuse. In looking after her clients Carrie is, by her own admission, also looking after herself (Beusman 2019). There is a sort of creative displacement here, through which the lawyer feels personally gratified when fighting for her clients.

Working within the law, Carrie has found a way to project her feelings of shame without resorting to destruction and disproportionality. The people whom she challenges in court have humiliated her clients; part of her task, as she sees it, is to shame those people (or their legal representatives) for having shamed her clients. She has spoken passionately of the joy that comes with being "in the position of shaming the shamer for being so fucking shameful" (Turk 2018).

Determined to 'shame the shamer' and to secure compensation for the victim, Carrie has at times been frustrated by the limitations of the law as it stands. Her response has been to work to get the law changed. She continues to be fired up by the injustice of her own traumatic experiences with men who had violated and terrorised her. When a judge told her some years ago that these men were legally entitled to distribute her intimate photographs to friends, family, colleagues, peers and strangers because of the provisions of the First Amendment, she felt as if she had been punched. It was tantamount to being told that the retributive justice system was there to protect the perpetrator. Through her own experiences of pain, disappointment and struggle she has been able to understand the terror and desperation of her clients when they bring similar cases to her law practice.

Radically Different Revenge

One of her clients was a young gay man called Matthew who had met his ex-partner on the dating app Grindr. After the couple broke up, Matthew began to receive numerous visitors calling at his house, all expecting to have sex with him. When he said there had been some misunderstanding and that he did not want to have sex with them, some of the callers became abusive and threatening. It transpired that the ex-partner had placed the ads on Grindr as though they were from Matthew, providing his name and address and suggesting that he enjoyed aggressive sex, rape fantasies and orgies. His life became nightmarish, as more and more strangers turned up at his home angrily insisting on having sex with Matthew, often becoming threatening and abusive. Fearful for his safety, Matthew contacted Grindr to ask them to stop his ex from putting up the fake profiles that were bringing these strangers to his home. Grindr ignored Matthew's requests and pleas. Eventually Matthew contacted Carrie Goldberg's firm asking for help. Investigating what sort of pressure could be put on Grindr to help Matthew, Carrie found that a specific clause known as Section 230 of the Communications Decency Act of 1996 protects internet companies such as Grindr from any legal responsibility for any content that users post on their websites. It is this clause which allows the internet to be a free and open space for people to post fake dating profiles, death threats, hate speech and other dangerous, violent and threatening content online.

Carrie has taken on the challenge of suing Grindr for facilitating the 'attempted rape and murder scheme' that Matthew's ex-partner had engaged in. For the past two and a half years she has been working through the law courts in an attempt to get legal recognition of a website's responsibilities for the content which they allow to be posted. She has so far not succeeded, but remains committed to continue her fight on behalf of Matthew and for "future victims' rights to sue any tech company that knowingly, or recklessly, aids their abusers, and causes victims harm". It is easy to imagine that at some level the fight is also to satisfy Carrie's own need for payback and restoration.

(iii) Stalking the Bogeyman: David Holthouse's story

When David Holthouse was seven years old he was brutally raped by the teenage son of close family friends. It happened one evening when David and his parents were visiting their friends. While the adults were upstairs chatting, the teenager invited David down to the basement to play, but the playing quickly turned ugly and before long the older boy had backed David into a corner and ordered him to take off his trousers. After forcing David to stimulate him orally, the teenager raped David, covering the seven-year-old boy's head with a pillow in order to muffle the screams. David remembers being terrified, confused and in terrible pain. Before he left the room, the teenager told him that if he told anyone about what had happened he would come to his house in the middle of the night and 'gut him like a salmon'.

For years, David was tormented by the memory of what had happened, a memory of pain, helplessness and shame which festered in his mind. As he got older, he thought more and more about getting revenge on the man who had raped him. But the one thing he wanted even more than revenge was to protect his parents from the pain of knowing that their son had been raped by their friends' child while the parents were upstairs socialising. So he held on to the secret of what had been done to him while fantasising about taking revenge.

In his teens David worried about the possible long-term consequences of having been abused. He was alarmed by studies that he had read which highlighted the frequency with which those who were once abused become abusers themselves. He was terrified that one day he may want to abuse a child, and decided that if ever he began to feel the slightest desire to do this, he would kill himself and, in order to protect his parents, he would make his suicide look like an accident.

Meanwhile, David continued to fantasise about revenge. His shame and anger were very specifically related to the trauma of having been raped; the object of his revenge fantasies was specifically the older boy who had raped him. There would be no relief for David in taking revenge on anyone other than the rapist himself. His urge to take revenge was bolstered, and in some ways rationalised, by David's concerns that the rapist might present a very real threat to other young boys. He felt he had both a desire and a responsibility to kill the rapist. He entertained thoughts of shooting him, of stabbing him, of bashing in his head and of carving out his heart. And the more he thought about the risk the rapist posed to others, the more he wanted to kill him, "to just walk right up to him in a secluded place and scrape him from this world like a piece of dog shit off my shoe" (Holthouse 2004).

Outwardly, David's life had moved on. He finished university and began working as a journalist. He left his home town in Alaska, and relocated to Arizona and later to Denver, Colorado. Shortly after moving to Denver, David heard from his parents that the son of their good friends – the person who had raped David some 25 years earlier – was also living in the Denver area. The news that the rapist was living somewhere in the vicinity came as a shock and reawakened the pain that had never really left his mind. He now became fixated on his desire to kill the man. What had previously been a fantasy now became a concrete plan (James 2013).

In 2003 David travelled back to Phoenix, Arizona in order to buy a gun from an illegal dealer so as to avoid having to get a license for the gun. This precaution would ensure that when he killed the rapist there would be nothing that could link him with the murder weapon. He was confident that he would never be considered a murder suspect, as there was nothing linking him to the rapist. After buying the gun, David returned to Denver, ready to kill his erstwhile assailant.

A year later, looking back to this time in his life, David acknowledged that, although he had been telling himself that he was going to kill the man in order to protect other children, the truth was that "more than anything else, I think I just wanted to shoot the son of a bitch". With hindsight, David thought he had been "a little insane" to plan to kill the rapist instead of bringing out into the open the terrible secret that this man had raped him when he was a little boy. David looked back on his 'insanity' with empathy, however, knowing that what had held him back from sharing his terrible secret was, more than anything else, a deep sense of shame, and a deep reluctance to let his parents find out what had happened.

What David's conscious mind had forgotten however was that many years ago he had in fact shared his secret with a diary he had written at the age of 10, just three years after the rape. And it was this which ultimately prevented him from shooting the rapist. In amongst the 10-year-old David's thoughts about his dying grandfather and his performance in a Little League match, was his description of the rape, and thoughts about what he would do if he were ever to encounter the rapist when he was a grown man. He wrote, "Will I smile and shake his hand and pretend nothing happened? Or will I punch him in the face?" but, in the event, the adult David did neither of those things.

Before he had time to carry out his plan to shoot the rapist, David received a telephone call from his mother. She told him that while clearing out the house she had found his childhood diary and read it, and she wondered if what he had written about the rape was true. Shocked, and perhaps in some ways relieved that the truth was finally out, David told his mother it was true. He said he would fly out to see his parents as soon as possible so that they could talk about what had happened all those years ago. In the meantime, however, his mother wrote to the rapist's parents telling them about the rape, and warning them that their son might be a danger to other young children. When David found out what his mother had done, he knew he could no longer go through with his plan to kill the rapist because he would now be a prime suspect in the murder case.

Although David may not consciously have remembered writing about the rape in his diary, it is possible that somewhere in his *unconscious* mind there was not only some knowledge of the diary but also a wish that someone – his mother – would find and read it, and save him from having to go through with an action that one part of him yearned for, but another part thought was insane. It is difficult to know for certain whether this was the case, just as we cannot know for sure if David would have dropped his plan to kill the rapist even if his mother *had not* read the diary and subsequently contacted the rapist's parents.

In recounting his story in the Colorado news weekly *Westword* (on which most of my account of David's experience is based), David makes it clear that for many years he was sustained by fantasies of revenge that involved killing the man who had raped him, and making him suffer the pain and shame that he had inflicted on David all those years ago. And yet something else comes through in his account which is that David's ability to reflect deeply on his own thoughts and actions ultimately counteracted his desire for physical revenge. At some level David knew that a big part of what he was struggling with was the shame that had haunted him in all the years following the rape; and he also knew that murdering the rapist would not alleviate this shame. Like Martin Greenfield, David was able to distinguish between what could be called physical and metaphysical revenge. Aware at some level of the limitations of the former, he ultimately opted for the latter as being of greater value to his sense of well-being.

Nevertheless, David did have vivid fantasies of destructive, physical revenge. These fantasies played an important role for a number of reasons. Firstly, they enabled David to direct his hatred and anger towards the rapist, rather than onto himself which may have led to dangerous acts of self-harm. Secondly, they buoyed him to some extent and prevented him from sinking into feelings of abject powerlessness, which would have intensified the feelings of shame that he was struggling with. Thirdly, and crucially, fantasies of physical revenge can provide the time and space necessary for working through the underlying feelings of anger, shame and pain, thereby paving the way for metaphysical revenge (Goldberg 2004).

Having decided to forego his plan to kill the rapist, David knew he still needed revenge. In some ways shooting the man could have been easier than confronting him about what he had done, but David decided he had to take this more difficult approach in order to feel relieved and vindicated. David wrote a letter to the rapist in which he referred explicitly to the rape incident, and said it was time for them to meet to talk it over. It was not an invitation; it was a demand that they should have the "uncomfortable conversation" that needed to be had. To his surprise, David heard back almost immediately from the rapist who agreed to meet. When they came face to face, the rapist apologised repeatedly for what he had done, and assured David that it was the one and only time he had ever done such a thing, and that he had never sexually assaulted any other child either before or after he had raped David. When David asked his assailant why he had done it, the rapist could not give him an answer, apart from once again expressing his sorrow and regret at having raped David. David listened as the rapist spoke. Writing about it afterwards he explains very movingly the shift in his revenge feelings:

When I was still planning to kill the man [that] I was now sitting beside on the 16th Street mall, my plan was to walk up, [and] say, "… You raped me when I was seven," and then pop, one slug to the crotch, let him writhe, kick him over, hold him down with my foot and then pop, pop, pop, three to the back of the head, lights out.

I knew that if I gave him time to talk, I might not pull the trigger – and sure enough, as soon as I exchanged a few sentences with him, I didn't want to shoot him at all, because I saw him as a frightened, damaged man. He wasn't the Bogeyman anymore. He was real. He begged my forgiveness. He swore I was the only one. (Holthouse 2004)

David was aware that the rapist might be lying, but he chose to believe him. After so many years, David had been able to regain a sense of self. He recovered from the shame and the pain he had lived with for so long, and he saw his aggressor for what he was: a damaged man who had begged for forgiveness. And so they finished their conversation, and said goodbye, and David watched as the rapist "blended into the crowd". Having heard the rapist's apology, and his insistence that there had never been any other victims, David decided to leave things as they were. He no longer even felt the need to expose the rapist publicly for what he was.

Instead, David wrote his story, first for the Denver news weekly *Westword* and later, together with theatre director Markus Potter, he turned the story into a stage play which was performed to critical acclaim in a number of theatres including off-Broadway in New York, at Southwark Playhouse in London, and at the Old Fitzroy Theatre in Sydney, Australia. The *New York Times* described the play as "Chilling. Heartbreaking. Breathtaking." and the *Sunday Times* wrote that it was "Brave and unflinching, intense and tightly executed…[a] challenging and thought-provoking piece of theatre that needs to be told". In writing his story, and in developing it into a stage play, David was able to present to the world what had happened, and to acquire witnesses not only to his suffering but, more importantly, witnesses to the heinous evil that his assailant had been capable of. In showing the rapist to the world in this way, David was able to satisfy his urge for revenge without physically attacking and killing the rapist.

This could have been the end of the story, but it was not. What happened next may have been a simple twist of fate, or an example of the surprising power of our unconscious minds. In writing about his childhood experience, David had been careful to protect the identity of the rapist. He did not at any time mention the rapist's name and he gave the rapist's age as 17, when in truth he had been 14. But by describing the rapist as a star athlete at the local high school and mentioning that he had at one time been profiled in the local newspaper, David unwittingly provided enough clues to indicate who the rapist was.

Almost eleven years after writing to the rapist and confronting him face to face, David was in Alaska at a public meeting where he was sharing his story. After the meeting, two people approached David to say they thought they might know of other victims of the rapist. When they told David who they thought the rapist was, David realised that they were probably telling the truth about there being other victims, and further research verified their stories. This new information flooded David with a range of emotions, including relief from finally knowing the truth about the rapist. He felt now that he was fully justified in publicly naming – and shaming – the rapist, which he subsequently did in the local newspaper. Doing this meant for David that he could "just finally tell on him, just ...finally give that 7-year-old a voice and tell on him" (Phu 2015)[19].

(iv) "Sometimes painting is the best revenge"[20]: Artemisia Gentileschi's story

In recent years there has been a growing interest in the work of the seventeenth century artist, Artemisia Gentileschi. Widely recognised as an exceptionally gifted baroque painter, she is also seen by some as an early

---

19 Because of the statute of limitations on child rape (which was ten years), and because victims who came after David have been reluctant to speak out, the rapist is still free and, quite possibly, still abusing and violating children.

20 Quote taken from the back cover of Jonathan Jones's excellent biography, *Artemisia Gentileschi* (2020).

feminist icon and even an early forerunner of the #MeToo movement. Whether one can attach a twenty-first century label to a seventeenth century figure is moot. What is less arguable is that Artemisia Gentileschi was a remarkably successful artist in an era when very few women became professional painters. Her success was due not only to her extraordinary talent and creative imagination, but also to her strength of character and ambition. These attributes stood her in good stead when she took a singular sort of metaphysical revenge against the man who raped her.

Artemisia Gentileschi was born in Rome in 1593 to the painter Orazio Gentileschi and his wife Prudentia Montone. Unlike her three younger brothers, Artemisia showed an early aptitude for painting which her father was eager to foster, even though painting was not considered a likely profession for a woman. After Artemisia's mother died in 1605 Orazio continued to encourage his daughter to paint, introducing her to some of his fellow painters, including the great Caravaggio and the lesser artist, Agostino Tassi, who worked together with Orazio on numerous frescoes, including some that had been commissioned by the Pope. A regular visitor at the Gentileschi household, one day Tassi found a way to divert the attention of Artemisia's chaperone and, alone in the room with 18-year -old Artemisia, he overwhelmed her with force and raped her. Artemisia's pain was heavily compounded by her dismay at having lost her virginity, which in most circumstances would mean losing the prospect of a good marriage. After the rape, however, Tassi promised Artemisia that he would marry her. She accepted this as a pragmatic solution to what could otherwise have caused serious social and financial problems for the entire family. Artemisia maintained a sexual relationship with Tassi for a number of months in the expectation that this courtship would end in marriage, but it soon emerged that Tassi was already married and had no intention of marrying Artemisia (Cohen 2000). The trauma of having been raped and the worry about having lost her virginity were deepened by the shame and rage at having been tricked into believing Tassi's promise of marriage. Nine months after the rape, Orazio took Tassi to court for having raped his daughter[21].

---

21 A fuller account of these events is available in Jonathan Jones's short but excellent book *Artemisia Gentileschi*.

In her masterful study of Artemisia's life and work, Mary Garrard provides an English translation of the testimony presented at Tassi's rape trial of 1612 (Garrard 1989). The records show that, on the order of the court, Artemisia was examined by midwives who confirmed that she was no longer a virgin. When questioned, Artemisia supported her father's charge that Tassi had raped her, and added that Tassi had also promised to marry her. Artemisia described her attempts to fight off Tassi: unable to push him off of her because he was physically too strong, and unable to scream because he had a hand over her mouth, she scratched his face, pulled his hair and grabbed his penis so tightly that, as she is reported to have put it, she "even removed a piece of flesh". Immediately after the rape, Artemisia grabbed a knife and told Tassi she wanted to kill him, to which he replied, presumably tauntingly, "here I am". Undaunted, Artemisia describes how she then threw the knife at him, wounding him slightly on the chest. It was at this point, as Artemisia was crying, that Tassi had falsely promised that he would marry her.

Tassi denied all of the charges, just as he had denied charges of incest with his sister-in-law in an earlier court case of 1611. When a key witness for the prosecution in the rape trial (Giovanni Battista Stiattesi) claimed that Tassi had earlier arranged for his wife to be murdered, Tassi denied this too. Tassi repeatedly refuted everything that Artemisia claimed in court. Knowing that Tassi was more likely to be believed than she, simply by virtue of being a man, Artemisia agreed to undergo physical torture in order to prove that she was telling the truth. Accordingly, a *sibille*[22] was wrapped around her fingers and tightened with ever-increasing pressure as her interrogators tried to establish if she was telling the truth about Tassi. As the torture was applied, Artemisia is reported to have cried out, "it's true, it's true, it's true". Eventually the court found in Artemisia's favour. Yet there is no record of Tassi ever having been sentenced to any punishment, a fact widely attributed to the protection Tassi enjoyed thanks to being one of the Pope's favoured artists (Jones 2016).

---

22 A *sibille* was a primitive torture device which worked along the same lines as thumb screws.

The rape trial must have been a harrowing experience for Artemisia Gentileschi, one which was fraught with shame and pain. In addition to being subjected to the midwives' examination of her hymen, the physical pain of the *sibille* torture, and the anxiety about losing her social standing due to having had sexual intercourse with a man who had not subsequently married her, there was the shame of having some of the most private aspects of her life exposed to one and all. At one point Artemisia was asked to tell the court whether she had bled after the rape, and she was obliged to answer that at the time of the rape she had been having her menstrual period and was therefore unsure whether her blood was due to her period, or to the rape, or both. Having survived this and other humiliations during the trial, Artemisia was ultimately vindicated by the verdict and able to begin to restore her honour and therefore her reputation. Soon after the trial ended she married another painter, Pierantonio di Vincenzo Stiattesi (the brother of Giovanni Battista Stiattesi), and in 1613 the couple moved to Florence where they had five children, although only one of them survived to adulthood.

Artemisia Gentileschi was exceptional, both in terms of her achievements as a seventeenth-century woman, and as a Baroque woman artist. After moving to Florence she quickly acquired a number of wealthy patrons, and in 1616 she became one of the few women ever to be enrolled in the prestigious Accademia del Disegno. Supported by members of the powerful Medici family, her work found favour – and commissions – not only in Florence but also in Genoa, Venice and Naples. Some time after Artemisia and her husband moved to Florence, he disappeared from her life, but she was able to support and raise her daughter on her own, which was no mean feat for a seventeenth century female artist.

Many of the art historians, novelists and playwrights who have studied Artemisia Gentileschi's work consider her paintings after 1611 to have been significantly influenced by her experience of rape as well as the subsequent trial and its aftermath. It is difficult to know how far to attribute this influence to a conscious attempt on the part of the artist to communicate something of her past through her painting; or, conversely, to an unconscious process of sublimation. Either way, Artemisia brilliantly expressed through her paintings something of the trauma she had been through, and the pain and anger that had been stirred up in her by having been violated and then tricked by Tassi. Remarkably, while depicting different aspects of her trauma, she simultaneously communicates in her work her fierce determination not to be cowed or diminished in any way by her aggressor.

Judith Beheading Holofernes
Artemisia Gentileschi 1620 c.
Uffizi, Florence

It is difficult to look at Artemisia's celebrated painting of *Judith Beheading Holofernes* without being powerfully affected. The painting is based on the Old Testament story of Judith who, by tricking the Assyrian General Holofernes, was able to foil his plans to destroy the Jewish city of Bethulia. The story goes that, knowing Holofernes desired her, Judith first flirted with him, then plied him with drink and, once he had drunkenly passed out, she decapitated him and carried his head away in a basket. It is hardly surprising that this astonishing bible story has inspired a number of painters, from Caravaggio in the late sixteenth century to Gustav Klimt in the early twentieth century. Each rendition is powerful in its own way, but none more so than Artemisia's.

Artemisia twice painted *Judith Beheading Holofernes*. Although the two paintings are in many ways similar, it is the second one (which hangs at the Uffizi in Florence) which is the more powerful of the two. In it, Judith is portrayed as physically powerful and mentally determined, absolutely unwavering in what she is doing – which is sawing away at Holofernes' neck with a long sword. Judith, whose face in the painting bears a striking resemblance to Artemisia's, appears to be unperturbed by the blood spraying up from the wound and trickling down the white bedsheets.

As mentioned above, Artemisia had been subjected during her trial to an intrusive examination to establish that her hymen had been broken, and she had been forced to answer questions about her menstrual blood. It is hard to ignore the connection between these experiences and her painting which shows Holofernes looking terrified and powerless, as he loses *his* blood and his life at the hands of this determined woman and her loyal maidservant who resolutely holds Holofernes down so that Judith can do her just work. Although the painting is an effective representation of the Bible story of Judith and Holofernes, it has also been interpreted as an act of revenge for the rape, particularly as it contrasts so strikingly with the works of other artists who, in representing the story of Judith and Holofernes, have focused on Judith's beauty and courage rather than on the gruesome minutiae of the act of killing Holofernes[23].

In a less well-known artwork that Artemisia painted around 1620, she depicts the story of Jael and Sisera. Like many bible stories, this one is open to diverse interpretations. Jael – a heroine in the Old Testament for having delivered Israel from the troops of King Jabin – was so beautiful that even hearing her voice would make men lust after her. Jabin's military commander, Sisera, was fleeing the enemy and approached Jael seeking refuge, asking if he could enter her tent. For some, 'entering her tent' is understood as a metaphor for having sexual intercourse with her. For others, it is a more straightforward and literal account of what happened. Views differ correspondingly on what exactly happened next. According to one view, Sisera 'entered the tent' in the sense of having had intercourse with Jael, then had a drink, and promptly fell asleep. An alternative interpretation is that he literally entered the tent in which Jael lived, whereupon she plied him with drink, after which he insisted on sexual intercourse before falling asleep. Either way, Artemisia's painting captures a moment after Sisera has 'entered the tent' and has fallen asleep. Jael's hand is raised, ready to hammer a tent peg into Sisera's head. Is this an act of revenge for Sisera's sexual aggression? Or is it an act of heroism to save the Israelites? Maybe it is both. In any event, it is easy to see why this relatively neglected bible story inspired Artemisia Gentileschi. Whereas previous painters had presented Jael as a beautiful but treacherous temptress, Artemisia shows her to be a strong and determined woman, ready to do what was necessary to defeat the violent and dissolute Sisera.

---

23 Interestingly, Garrard notes that this version of Judith Slaying Holofernes was for several centuries banished to the dark corners of the Uffizi. She suggests this might have been partly because of the terror and shame it might have aroused in men, for whom the idea of being defeated by a woman was difficult to countenance.

Jael and Sisera
Artemisia Gentileschi 1620
Szépművészeti Múzeum/ Museum of Fine Arts, Budapest, 2020

In around 1615–1617, Artemisia completed what was to become one of her best-known paintings which is her *Self-Portrait as St Catherine of Alexandria*. At first sight there is no obvious reference to violence in this (self-) portrait of a rather solemn and pensive St Catherine, but a closer look shows how the painting speaks deeply of Artemisia's own pain, as well as her ability to survive and rise above it. In a sense, this is among the most sublime of her paintings, not least because of the extent to which her vengeance is sublimated in her artistic achievement. In the painting, Artemisia/St Catherine is almost but not quite looking at you, as though her mind is elsewhere. One wonders what she is thinking of, what preoccupies this young and earnest woman. A clue is in the story of St Catherine of Alexandria, who had rebuked the emperor of Alexandria for his paganism and his cruelty. She was then punished for her act of bravery by being brutally tortured and imprisoned, and eventually put to death.

Self-Portrait as Saint Catherine of Alexandria
Artemisia Gentileschi 1616
© The National Gallery, London

Initially Catherine was going to be killed slowly and painfully on a spiked breaking wheel, but she evaded the wheel and was instead beheaded. So once again, here is a noble and just woman who was cruelly abused and unjustly violated. Yet this painting is as much about survival as it is about injustice: it is St Catherine standing strong, next to a piece of the spiked wheel that failed to kill her, just as the *sibille* had failed to break Artemisia. The deep frown line between St Catherine's eyebrows hints both at thoughtfulness and pain, but she stands firm and vindicated. Artemisia's revenge is contained in, and expressed through, her remarkable act of survival, and her ability to express her life force through her artwork, saying 'I am here, you did not destroy me.'

Chapter Six
Final Thoughts: Radical Revenge in a Post-Truth World

Simone de Beauvoir struggled to come to terms with the fact that, although revenge often leaves "a taste of ashes in our mouths", we nevertheless seem to have an implacable desire to punish those who have harmed us. She attributed our proclivity for revenge to a deep-seated need for equivalence, expressed in the well-known biblical injunction to take an eye for an eye, and a tooth for a tooth. Acknowledging the enduring and yet mysterious appeal of talion, de Beauvoir suggested that somehow it "preserves some ancient magical aftertaste, gratifying who knows what dark god of symmetry, but it plainly answers a deep human need as well" (de Beauvoir 1946).

This book has linked the 'deep human need' for revenge to our instinct for self-preservation. In the very early stages of life, the self is experienced as the bodily self. At this stage, a harm to this physical self can be responded to with physical tit-for-tat. As the baby grows and develops, the sense of self and instinct for self-preservation become more complex and nuanced. They come to encompass the preservation of both the physical and metaphysical self. Chapter Two explained how a feeling such as shame, grievance or envy can in some instances be experienced as a profound, even existential, threat to the self. When this occurs, the person may feel that the only way to recover and protect their sense of self is through revenge: an act of retaliation in which the aggrieved person projects the feelings of shame or grievance onto the perceived aggressor.

Although revenge is often 'ordinary' in the sense of being one-off acts which are roughly proportionate to the harm that has been caused, in some cases it is manifestly disproportionate in its relentlessness and/or its level of destructiveness. How can we account for these extreme acts of vengeance which disregard de Beauvoir's dark god of symmetry? The concept of radical revenge, with its psychoanalytic underpinnings, provides an answer to this otherwise perplexing question. For some people who are weighed down by traumatic experiences buried deep in their past and lodged in their psyche, a one-off incident which causes them shame or envy can take on an amplified significance. As a consequence, when they take revenge for the one-off incident, they may unconsciously also be trying to off-load their more deep-rooted sense of grievance and pain. What they may believe is equivalence is in reality unreasonable and disproportionate. It is, in other words, radical revenge.

Chapters Two, Three and Four showed how radical revenge is often targeted at people who may not have intended to cause harm or, in some cases, at people who have not *in reality* caused any harm at all. The failure to take account of intentionality or of culpability is a defining feature of radical revenge, and can be the result of ignorance, misunderstanding, delusion or paranoia.

Most of us experience occasional or fleeting delusional thoughts at one time or another. An alcoholic who depends on alcohol to get through the day may truly believe he can easily give up drink any time he chooses. Someone else may routinely try to avoid stepping on cracks in the pavement believing this will have important consequences for someone else's life. A third person might imagine that if no one knows how old they are, this will somehow slow down the ageing process. These sorts of delusory thoughts are not uncommon and are in principle reversible. By contrast, structured paranoid delusions that govern a person's way of being are much more difficult to give up because of their psychological function, which is to protect a disturbed mind from even greater disturbances that are buried deep in the person's internal world. Those internal disturbances, which are born out of early experiences of trauma or deprivation, need to be fended off through thinking that replaces reality with something that feels more manageable.

While paranoid delusions can serve this important purpose, they also bring a host of problems which can include a bent for radical revenge against what are perceived to be enemies. This was seen, for example, in the case of Elliot Rodger who saw people laughing at him when they were, in fact, minding their own business. He ended up shooting and killing his imagined tormentors (Chapter Two). It was also evident in the case of the troubled and vengeful internet troll who felt that Lindy West was shaming him when in reality all she had done was state publicly and confidently that she was happy with being a fat woman (Chapter Three). Delusion can also come into play in certain group dynamics. For example, under the influence of a strong group identity and led by a compelling demagogue, supporters of populist parties come to believe that certain groups in society must be punished, expelled or in some cases even killed in revenge for the harms they are falsely accused of causing (Chapter Four). Delusory thinking is often at the heart of acts of radical revenge, and is epitomised in the belief that the radical revenge is justified and that it is proportionate to the harm which the perpetrator believes has been caused.

In a paper written in 1924, Sigmund Freud distinguished between neurotic functioning and the delusional functioning of the psychotic mind. He noted that both neurosis and psychosis arise out of the conflict between the demands of a person's deep-rooted and largely unconscious wishes on the one hand, and the competing demands of reality on the other. In neurosis, the demands of reality generally prevail and disturbing unconscious wishes have to be repressed or otherwise defended against. Conversely, for the psychotic person, reality with all its painful associations is unbearable, and so he refashions reality in his mind in a way that allows for his wishes to prevail. An example might be a man who is plagued by a profound sense of vulnerability and powerlessness, and who wishes to expunge these feelings by completely dominating someone else, exercising violent power over them, and viciously forcing them to submit to his will. If he were neurotic, this man would ultimately accept the demands of reality (which prohibit these sorts of actions) and would (unconsciously) find some other way to defend himself against his insecurities. Conversely, the psychotic might commit rape, guided by a delusional belief that the woman had 'asked for it'.

In distinguishing between neurosis and psychosis, Freud took for granted that external reality is the significant non-variable, while the significant variable is the individual's mind and how it responds to that reality. But this assumption is no longer so straightforward in our post-truth world, where reality seems less certain and more variable than ever. Widespread distortion, deception and a flagrant disregard for truth have left many of us unsure about what is, and is not, true or real. The post-truth world feels psychotic at times: a world where reality appears to fluctuate according to the wishes of those who are in power.

President Trump frequently spoke of his wishes as though they were facts. For instance, shortly after his election in 2016 he claimed that he had won the popular vote (which he had not), that he had had the biggest electoral victory since President Reagan (he had not), and that the crowd of supporters attending his inauguration was the largest in US history (it was not). Although none of these claims were true, they were presented as an account of reality (McIntyre 2018). Whether Trump was lying or delusional, his false accounts of reality had significant consequences, not least in spreading confusion and uncertainty. A survey carried out in December 2016 found that 64% of US adults felt confused about the basic facts regarding current events (Pew Research Center 2017).

There has been a similar disregard for truth and reality in the UK. In 2016, when the country was in the throes of conflict over whether or not to leave the European Union (EU), much of the debate turned on the alleged economic benefits of leaving versus remaining in the EU. When representatives of the Leave Campaign were asked to justify their claim that leaving the EU would give Britain a saving of £350 million every week, they were hard pressed to do so. The UK Statistics Authority said the figure was misleading and had undermined public trust in official statistics to which the government's Justice Secretary – a prominent figure in the Leave camp – retorted, "people in this country have had enough of experts" (Mance 2016). In France, the far-right candidate Marine Le Pen stated as fact a spurious rumour which had recently circulated on Twitter that her liberal opponent Emmanuel Macron had stashed money away in a secret Caribbean bank account. In Germany, Chancellor Angela Merkel was falsely reported to have taken a selfie with one of the men accused of a terror attack in Brussels. In Nigeria, a fake Twitter account was set up in the name of one of the 2019 presidential candidates thanking the 'Association of

Nigerian Gay Men'" for their support, thereby ensuring the candidate would lose many of his potential voters. In Brazil there was so much disinformation swirling around during the 2018 election that even Facebook removed links to more than 30 fake news stories.

The distortion of truth and the dissemination of disinformation for political purposes has been with us for centuries but, unlike earlier times, it is no longer simply about the spread of propaganda and rumours from one person or community to another[24]. In the post-truth world, the deliberate and often intricate misleading of others is carried out with impunity on a vast scale via social media. Once the disinformation is put online by those seeking to manipulate popular perceptions of reality, others unwittingly perpetuate the process by 'liking' what they read, and disseminating it further. Another layer of doubt is added when these untruths are followed up with the dismissal of what is actually true as 'fake news'[25]. The result is widespread confusion about what is true or real. Whose word can I trust? The journalist or the politician? The expert or the person whose Facebook profile I like (but who may in fact be a bot)? Who has my interests at heart, and who is trying to manipulate me? These sorts of doubts about what is real and what is not, and the vast potential for paranoid ideation created by post-truth, have dire consequences for radical revenge.

Firstly, many of us who are filled with disconcerting doubts about the world around us will quite naturally yearn for some certainty. Social

---

24 See for instance David Coast's study Misinformation and Disinformation in Late Jacobean Court Politics *Journal of Early Modern History* 16 (2012): 335–354

25 Those who claim to seek the truth are sometimes the very people who mislead us. During the 2019 general election in Britain, the Conservative Party rebranded its Twitter account as 'factcheckUK', thereby deliberately creating the impression that the account belonged to a non-political organisation that was fact-checking the statements of British political parties. Statements posted on the account by the Conservative Party were prefixed with the term 'Fact'", while those of rival parties were depicted as questionable. When asked about this distortion during a television interview, one of the Party's most senior figures stated that "no one gives a toss about the social media cut and thrust": a candid statement about the contempt with which truth is held.

psychologists have developed what is called *uncertainty-identity theory* to explain how the search for certainty can motivate behaviours that people might not otherwise adopt. Studies have shown for example that many people resort to identifying themselves with a group in order to reduce their feelings of uncertainty. Groups provide a defined set of norms and values, and shared understandings of what is important, and in this way they offer a sense of stability and predictability (Hogg 2007). Hogg and Adelman show through empirical research that extremist groups are especially suited to providing the much sought-after certainty, because these groups tend to be clearly structured, with distinct roles and functions assigned to members and leaders (Hogg and Adelman 2013). Authoritarian leaders who introduce, implement, and uphold strict rules about what is and is not permissible will be admired and followed because of the certainty they seem to provide. It is in this context that a toxic cycle emerges whereby extremist leaders continue to propagate distorted messages and untruths about what is and is not real, thereby heightening insecurity and uncertainty, which in turn enhances their following amongst those who yearn for certainty. Radical revenge serves as the oil in the wheels of this toxic cycle: history shows us time and time again that extremist groups and leaders define themselves largely in terms of who their enemies are, and they perpetuate their existence by inciting and legitimising radical revenge against these alleged enemies.

Secondly, in an uncertain world, people who are susceptible to paranoid ideation will be drawn to conspiracy theories which offer coherent and convincing – but entirely untrue – accounts of disturbing and confusing events. Conspiracy theories often induce an element of anxiety and they deepen existing uncertainties, but at the same time they purport to offer clarity about who is (allegedly) to blame for current difficulties. For instance, in the 1980s when the HIV pandemic was spreading through the world and not much was yet known about the virus, one conspiracy theory suggested that HIV had been intentionally introduced by the World Health Organisation (WHO) into developing countries through infected supplies of the polio vaccine. This 'theory' bred a heightened mistrust not only of the polio vaccine, but of public health officials generally and WHO in particular. Although the theory was disproven, its impact was considerable, as shown in the drop in uptake for the polio vaccine in some parts of the world.

Another example of an anxiety-inducing conspiracy theory is the so-called 'false flag' theories which are particularly popular in far right circles. False flag theories are based on the notion that recent mass killings in the US, including acts of terrorism, are part of a government plot to take away personal freedoms. Tragedies such as the Boston marathon bombing in April 2013, and the school shooting at Sandy Hook Elementary School, are explained as having been orchestrated by the government to provide the authorities with an excuse for clamping down on civil liberties and restricting the individual's right to own and use guns[26]. These sorts of ideas can leave individuals confused and anxious, and searching for a sense of safety. They may turn for certainty to the very organisations and individuals who propagate these sorts of harmful myths and lies.

The implications of these sorts of conspiracy theories for radical revenge are profoundly worrying. Their seriousness is illustrated by the infamous Pizzagate incident. In December 2016 a 28-year-old man travelled from North Carolina to Washington DC and walked into the Comet Ping Pong pizza restaurant armed with a pistol and assault rifle. After telling customers to get out of his way, he searched the premises and then began to open fire. Unlike many other shootings, this was not in fact a case of an individual acting on a paranoid delusion. The shooter had read online that this pizza restaurant was being used by Hillary Clinton and other Democrats as a front for a child sex ring, and that the victims were being held in vaults beneath the shop. The shooter had believed the report and went to the premises to confront the evil (non-

---

26 In October 2019 the father of a six-year-old boy who had been killed at Sandy Hook won $450,000 in a lawsuit against a conspiracy theorist who had claimed that the Sandy Hook shooting had never occurred but instead was staged by the Obama administration in an attempt to enforce tighter gun controls.

existent) paedophiles. Post-truth society can expect more of these cases of revenge against imagined enemies as a result of the spread of disinformation, and the anxiety and insecurity which flows from it.

** ** ** ** **

Once we recognise that all acts of retaliation, payback and tit-for-tat are forms of revenge, we can appreciate how pervasive revenge is in our daily lives. This book has argued that our desire for revenge is part of our instinct for self-preservation, and as such it cannot simply be dismissed or disparaged. What we each *do* with the desire for revenge is what matters most, and this will vary from person to person, and case to case. We may let ourselves be satisfied with a fantasy of revenge, or we might displace the revenge onto an inanimate object. Where we feel compelled to get some sort of equivalence, we might delegate the punishment to lawyers and judges, or we may engage in acts of ordinary revenge that are more or less proportionate and take account of intention and causality. In exceptional cases, we may rise above the need to repay a harm with a harm and instead look for a radically different sort of revenge which allows for more creative ways of restoring our sense of self. And then there are the cases of radical revenge which are dark, destructive and disturbing. It is only by keeping a firm hold of a sense of reality and by accepting the limitations that reality places on us that we can keep the desire for radical revenge in the domain of wishes rather than actions.

References

Akhtar, S. (2014) Revenge: An Overview. In: S. Akhtar and H. Parens (eds.) *Revenge*. Lanham: Jason Aronson.

AP News (1999) Barton's Mother Sensed Problems. *AP News* 31 July. Available at: https://www.apnews.com/4ee33cbaf985ee6e16f203b615cd3696 (accessed 21 February 2019).

Arendt, H. (1951) *The Origins of Totalitarianism*. Reprint, New York: Harvest, Harcourt Publishing, 1976.

Axelrod, R. (1984) *The Evolution of Co-Operation*. Reprint, London: Penguin Books, 1990.

Balint, M. (1952) New Beginning and the Paranoid and the Depressive Syndromes. *International Journal of Psycho-analysis*, 33: 214–224.

Beusman, C. (2019) *The Lawyer Taking on 'Pervs, Psychos and Trolls'*. Available at: https://www.thecut.com/2019/06/how-carrie-goldberg-revenge-porn-lawyer-dresses-for-work.html (accessed 9 September 2019).

Bollas, C. (2018) *Meaning and Melancholia: Life in the Age of Bewilderment*. Abingdon: Routledge.

Bowlby, J. (1944) Forty-four Juvenile Thieves: Their Characters and Home-Life. *International Journal of Psycho-analysis*, 25: 19–53.

Browning, C. R. (1992) *Ordinary Men: Reserve Police Battalion 101 and the Final Solution in Poland*. Reprint, London: Penguin Books, 2001.

Campbell, D. (1994) Breaching the Shame Shield: Thoughts on the Assessment of Adolescent Child Sexual Abusers. *Journal of Child Psychotherapy*, 20(3): 309–326.

Campbell, D. (2014) Debt, Shame and Violence in Adolescence: Reactions to the Absent Father in the Film Bullet Boy. *International Journal of Psycho-analysis*, 95(5): 1011–1020.

Castelman, M. (2018) *Surprising new data from the world's most popular porn site*. Available at: https://www.psychologytoday.com/us/blog/all-about-sex/201803/surprising-new-data-the-world-s-most-popular-porn-site (accessed 12 May 2019).

Citron, D. K. (2014) *Hate Crimes in Cyberspace*. Cambridge: Harvard University Press.

Citron, D. K. and Franks, M. A. (2014) Criminalizing Revenge Porn *Wake Forest Law Review Vol. 49*. University of Maryland Legal Studies Research Paper. Available at: https://papers.ssrn.com/sol3/papers.cfm?abstract_id=2368946 (accessed 13 May 2019).

Cohen, E. S. (2000) The Trials of Artemisia Gentileschi: A Rape as History. *The Sixteenth Century Journal,* 31(1): 47–75.

Cooper, A. (ed.) (2002) *Sex and the Internet: a guidebook for clinicians*. New York: Brunner-Routledge.

Corn, D. (2016) *Donald Trump is Completely Obsessed with Revenge*. Available at https://www.motherjones.com/politics/2016/10/donald-trump-obsessed-with-revenge/ (accessed 12 November 2018).

Counts, D. A. (1987) Female Suicide and Wife Abuse in Cross Cultural Perspective. *Suicide and Life Threatening Behavior,* 17(3): 194–204.

Crockett, M. J., Özdemir, Y, and Fehr, E. (2014) The Value of Vengeance and the Demand for Deterrence. *Journal of Experimental Psychology*, 143(6): 2279–2286.

Cullen, D. (2019a) Changing the Story. *The Guardian* 9 February 2019.

Cullen, D. (2019b) *Columbine*. London: riverrun.

Curato, N. (2016) Politics of Anxiety, Politics of Hope: Penal Populism and Duterte's Rise to Power. *Journal of Current Southeast Asian Affairs* 35(3): 91–109. Available at: https://journals.sagepub.com/doi/full/10.1177/186810341603500305 (accessed 1 July 2019).

de Beauvoir, S. (1946) *An Eye for an Eye*. Now and Then eBook Collection (accessed 20 October 2019).

de Quervain, D. J-F., Fischbacher, U., Treyer, V., Schellhammer, M., Schnyder, U., Buck, A. and Fehr, E. (2004) The Neural Basis of Altruistic Punishment. *Science* 305(5688): 1254–1258.

Dewey, C. (2015*) The revenge pornographers next door*. Available at: https://www.washingtonpost.com/news/the-intersect/wp/2015/03/19/the-revenge-pornographers-next-door/?utm_term=.80a8f1ced0f8 (accessed 21 May 2019).

Donner, C. M. (2016) The Gender Gap and Cybercrime: An Examination of College Students' Online Offending. *Victims and Offenders*, 11(4): 556–577.

Doonan, B. C. (2006) *Murder at the Office: a twisted outcast with a deadly agenda and two loaded guns*. Far Hills: Expanding Horizons.

D'Ovidio, R. and Doyle, J. (2003) A Study on Cyberstalking. *FBI Law Enforcement Bulletin*, No. 10. March 2003.

Dunbar-Ortiz, R. (2018) *Loaded: A Disarming History of the Second Amendment*. San Francisco: City Lights Books.

Dundes Renteln, A. (1988) A Cross-Cultural Approach to Validating International Human Rights: The Case of Retribution Tied to Proportionality. In: D.L. Cingranelli (ed.) *Human Rights: Theory and Measurement*. Basingstoke: Macmillan Press.

Elster, J. (1990) Norms of Revenge. *Ethics*, 100(4): 862–885.

Fagone, J. (2015) *The Serial Swatter*. Available at: (https://www.nytimes.com/2015/11/29/magazine/the-serial-swatter.html) (accessed 10 June 2019).

Fehr, E. and Gächter, S. (1999) *Cooperation and Punishment in Public Goods Experiments*. Institute for Empirical Research in Economics, University of Zurich, Working Paper No. 10: CESifo Working Paper Series No. 183. Available at https://ssrn.com/abstract=203194 (accessed 18 June 2019).

References

Ferenczi, S. (1920) Letter from Sándor Ferenczi to Sigmund Freud, 18 April 1920. *The Correspondence of Sigmund Freud and Sándor Ferenczi* Vol 3, 1920–1933: 15–17. Reprint, Cambridge: Harvard University Press, 2000.

Fisk, R. (2010) *The crimewave that shames the world*. Available at: https://www. independent.co.uk/voices/commentators/fisk/robert-fisk-the-crimewave-that-shames-the-world-2072201.html (Accessed 22 August 2019).

Freedland, J. (2008) *Revenge*. Available at: https://www.theguardian.com/world/2008/ jul26/second.world.war (accessed 19 September 2019).

French, P. A. (2001) *The Virtues of Vengeance*. Lawrence: University Press of Kansas.

Freud, S. (1905) Three Essays on the Theory of Sexuality. *The Standard Edition of the Complete Psychological Works of Sigmund Freud* Volume VII. London: Hogarth Press.

Freud, S. (1910) 'Wild' Psycho-analysis. *The Standard Edition of the Complete Psychological Works of Sigmund Freud* Volume XI. London: Hogarth Press.

Freud, S. (1914) On Narcissism: An Introduction. *The Standard Edition of the Complete Psychological Works of Sigmund Freud* Volume XIV. London: Hogarth Press.

Freud, S. (1920) Beyond the Pleasure Principle. *The Standard Edition of the Complete Psychological Works of Sigmund Freud* Volume XVIII. London: Hogarth Press.

Freud, S. (1921) Group Psychology and the Analysis of the Ego. *The Standard Edition of the Complete Psychological Works of Sigmund Freud* Volume XVIII. London: Hogarth Press.

Freud, S. (1924a) Neurosis and Psychosis. *The Standard Edition of the Complete Psychological Works of Sigmund Freud* Volume XIX. London: Hogarth Press.

Freud, S. (1924b) The Loss of Reality in Neurosis and Psychosis. *The Standard Edition of the Complete Psychological Works of Sigmund Freud* Volume XIX. London: Hogarth Press.

Freud, S. (1925) Negation. *The Standard Edition of the Complete Psychological Works of Sigmund Freud* Volume XIX. London: Hogarth Press.

Freud, S. (1938) Splitting of the Ego in the Process of Defence. *The Standard Edition of the Complete Psychological Works of Sigmund Freud,* Volume XXIII. London: Hogarth Press.

Frijda, N. H. (2009) The Lex Talionis: On Vengeance. In: T. H. M. Van Goozen, N. E. Van de Poll, and J. A. Sergeant (eds.) *Emotions: Essays on Emotion Theory.* New York: Routledge.

Garrard, M. D. (1989) *Artemisia Gentileschi*. Princeton: Princeton University Press.

Gegax, T. T. (1999) *'It's a bad trading day… And it's about to get –.'* Available at https:// www.newsweek.com/its-bad-trading-day-and-its-about-get-165768 (accessed 21 February 2019).

Glasser, M. (1985) 'The Weak Spot' – Some Observations on Male Sexuality. *International Journal of Psycho-analysis*, 66: 405–414.

Goldberg, C. (2019) *Nobody's Victim: Fighting Psychos, Stalkers, Pervs and Trolls*. London: Virago.

Goldberg, J. (2004) Fantasies of Revenge and the Stabilization of the Ego: Acts of Revenge and the Ascension of Thanatos. *Modern Psychoanalysis,* 29(1): 3–21.

Graham-Dixon, A. (2010) Five things to know about Caravaggio. *Financial Times* 10 July 2010.

Greenfield, M. (2014) *Measure of a Man: A Memoir.* Washington DC: Regnery History.

Gu, J. (2020) Deadliest Mass Shootings Are Often Preceded by Violence at Home. Available at: https://www.bloomberg.com/graphics/2020-mass-shootings-domestic-violence-connection/ (accessed 1 July 2020).

Gun Violence Archive 2019. Available at: https://www.gunviolencearchive.org (accessed 12 September 2018).

Hagan, C. R., Podlogar, M. C., and Joiner, T. E. (2015) Murder-Suicide: Bridging the Gap between Mass Murder, Amok, and Suicide. *Journal of Aggression, Conflict and Peace Research*, 7(3): 179–186.

Hall, M. and Hearn, J. (2018) *Revenge Pornography: Gender, Sexualities and Motivations.* Abingdon: Routledge.

Halpert-Zamir, L. (2018) Holocaust Literature as Metaphysical Revenge. In: V. S. Chauhan and L. Halpert-Zamir (eds.) *Eight Faces of Revenge.* Brill Rodopi, e-book. Available at: https://brill.com/view/title/35660?rskey=b1y8Gb&result=1 (accessed 11 September 2019).

Hannaford, A. (2018) *We asked 12 mass killers: 'What would have stopped you?'* Available at: https://www.gqmagazine.co.uk/article/mass-shootings-in-america-interviews (accessed 15 November 2018).

Hardaker, C. (2013) *What is turning so many young men into internet trolls?* Available at: https://www.theguardian.com/media/2013/aug/03/how-to-stop-trolls-social-media (accessed 18 June 2019).

Harding, D., Mehta, J., and Newman K. (2003) No Exit: Mental Illness, Marginality, and School Violence in West Paducah, Kentucky. In: Moore, M. H., Petrie, C. V., Braga, A. A., and McLaughlin, B. L. (eds.) *Deadly Lessons: Understanding Lethal School Violence.* Washington DC: The National Academies Press.

Hochschild, A. R. (2016) *Strangers in Their Own Land: Anger and Mourning on the American Right.* New York: The New Press.

Hogg, M. A. (2007) Uncertainty-Identity Theory. *Advances in Experimental Social Psychology*, 39: 69–126.

Hogg, M. A. and Adelman, J. (2013) Uncertainty-Identity Theory: Extreme Groups, Radical Behaviour, and Authoritarian Leadership. *Journal of Social Issues*, 69(3): 436–454.

Holthouse, D. (2004) *Stalking the Bogeyman.* Available at: https://www.westword.com/news/stalking-the-bogeyman-5079302 (accessed 5 September 2019).

Horney, K. (1948) The Value of Vindictiveness. *The American Journal of Psychoanalysis*, 8(1): 3–12.

Jackson, J. C., Choi, V. K., and Gelfand, M. J. (2019) Revenge: A Multilevel Review and Synthesis. *Annual Review of Psychology*, 70: 319–345.

References

James, S. D. (2013) *Reporter Once Plotted to Murder Man Who Raped Him at 7.* Available at: https://abcnews.go.com/Health/stalking-bogeyman-raped-david-holthouse-plots-kill-assailant/story?id=18825105 (accessed 3 September 2019).

Jones, J. (2016) More savage than Caravaggio: the woman who took revenge in oil. *The Guardian* 4 October 2016.

Jones, J. (2020) *Artemisia Gentileschi.* London: Lawrence King.

Kaufman, W. R. P. (2013) *Honor and Revenge: A Theory of Punishment.* New York: Springer.

Kelleher, M. D. (1997) *Flashpoint: The American Mass Murderer.* Westport: Praeger.

Khan, M. R. (1963) The Concept of Cumulative Trauma. In: M. Khan (1974) *The Privacy of the Self.* London: Karnac.

Kris, E. (1941) The 'Danger' of Propaganda. *American Imago*, 2(1): 3–42.

Krugman, P. (2018) *The Angry White Male Caucus.* Available at: https://www.nytimes.com/2018/10/01/opinion/kavanaugh-white-male-privilege.html (accessed 8 July 2019).

Lane, R. C. (1995) The revenge motive: A developmental perspective on the life cycle and treatment process. *Psychoanalytic Review*, 82(1): 41–64.

Langman, P. (2009) *Why Kids Kill: Inside the Minds of School Shooters.* New York: St Martins Griffin.

Langman, P. (2014) Transcript of Elliot Rodger's "Retribution" Video. Available at: https://schoolshooters.info/sites/default/files/rodger_video_1.0.pdf (accessed 12 January 2019).

Langman, P. (2015) *School Shooters: Understanding High School, College, and Adult Perpetrators.* Lanham: Rowman and Littlefield.

Lansky, M. (1987) Shame and Domestic Violence. In: D.L. Nathanson (ed.) *The Many Faces of Shame.* New York: Guildford Press.

Lansky, M. (2007) Unbearable Shame, Splitting, and Forgiveness in the Resolution of Vengefulness. *Journal of the American Psychoanalytic Association*, 55(2): 571–593.

Laplanche, J. and Pontalis, J-P. (1973) *The Language of Psychoanalysis.* Reprint, London: Karnac, 2006.

Levendowski, A. (2014) *Our best weapon against revenge porn: copyright law?* Available at https://www.theatlantic.com/technology/archive/2014/02/our-best-weapon-against-revenge-porn-copyright-law/283564/ (accessed 20 May 2019).

Lewis, H. B. (1987) Shame and the Narcissistic Personality. In: D. L. Nathanson (ed.) *The Many Faces of Shame.* New York: Guildford Press.

Lichtenberg, J. (2001) The Ethics of Retaliation. *Philosophy and Public Policy Quarterly*, 21(4): 4–8.

Lukes, S. (2008) *Moral Relativism.* London: Profile.

Mance, H. (2016) Britain has had enough of experts, says Gove. Available at: https://www.ft.com/content/3be49734-29cb-11e6-83e4-abc22d5d108c (accessed 12 December 2019).

Manne, K. (2019) *Down Girl: The Logic of Misogyny.* UK: Penguin.

Mantilla, K. (2015) *Gendertrolling*. Santa Barbara: Praeger.

Marongiu, P. and Newman, G. (1987) *Vengeance*. Totowa: Rowman and Littlefield.

McCullough, M. E. (2008) *Beyond Revenge: The Evolution of the Forgiveness Instinct.* San Francisco: Jossey-Bass.

McCullough, M. E., Kurzban, R. and Tabak, B. A. (2013) Cognitive Systems for Revenge and Forgiveness. *Behavioral and Brain Sciences*, 36: 1–58.

McIntyre, L. (2018) *Post-Truth*. Cambridge: MIT Press.

Money-Kyrle, R. (1941) The Psychology of Propaganda. In: D. Meltzer and E. O'Shaughnessy (eds.) *The Collected Papers of Roger Money-Kyrle.* London: Karnac & Harris Meltzer Trust, 2015.

Morrison, A. P. and Lansky, M. R. (2014) Shame and Envy. In: L. Wurmser and H. Jarass (eds.) *Jealousy and Envy.* New York: Routledge.

Mullen, P. E. (2004) The Autogenic (Self-Generated) Massacre. *Behavioral Sciences and the Law*, 22: 311–323.

Neumann, S. (1938) The Rule of the Demagogue. *American Sociological Review*, Vol. 3(4): 487–498.

Nussbaum, M. (2010) Objectification and Internet Misogyny. In: S. Levmore and M. Nussbaum (eds.) *The Offensive Internet.* Cambridge: Harvard University Press.

Ogden, T. O. (2010) On Three Forms of Thinking: Magical Thinking, Dream Thinking, and Transformative Thinking. *The Psychoanalytic Quarterly*, 79(2): 317–347.

Pew Research Center (2017) Key Trends Shaping Technology in 2017. Available at: https://www.pewresearch.org/fact-tank/2017/12/28/key-trends-shaping-technology-in-2017/ (accessed 18 December 2019).

Pew Research Center (2019) Race in America 2019. Available at: https://www.pewsocialtrends.org/2019/04/09/race-in-america-2019/ (accessed 8 December 2019).

Phillips, W. (2015) *This Is Why We Can't Have Nice Things*. Cambridge: MIT Press.

Phu, L. (2015) *How David Holthouse decided to name the 'Bogeyman'*. Available at: https://www.alaskapublic.org/2015/06/26/how-david-holthouse-decided-to-name-the-bogeyman/ (accessed 14 July 2019).

Piers, G. and Singer, M. B. (1953) *Shame and Guilt.* Reprint, Mansfield Centre: Martino Publishing, 2015.

Pinker, S. (2011) *The Better Angels of Our Nature: A History of Violence and Humanity.* Reprint, London: Penguin, 2012.

Powell, A. and Henry, N. (2017) *Sexual Violence in a Digital Age.* London: Palgrave.

Rippon, G. (2019a) *The Gendered Brain: the New Neuroscience that Shatters the Myth of the Female Brain.* London: Bodley Head.

Rippon, G. (2019b) The truth about male and female brains: Do we really think differently? *New Scientist,* 2 March.

Rodger, E. (undated) *My Twisted World: The Story of Elliot Rodger*. Available at: https://schoolshooters.info/sites/default/files/rodger_my_twisted_world.pdf (accessed 13 October 2018).

References

Rosenfeld, H. (1987) *Impasse and Interpretation*. Reprint, Hove: Brunner-Routledge, 2002.

Rycroft, C. (1968) *Critical Dictionary of Psychoanalysis*. Reprint, London: Penguin Books, 1995.

Rycroft, C. (1972) *Wilhelm Reich*. Viking: New York.

Sack, K. (1999) *Shootings in Atlanta: The Overview; Killer Confessed in a Letter Spiked with Rage*. Available at https://www.nytimes.com/1999/07/31/us/shootings-in-atlanta-the-overview-killer-confessed-in-a-letter-spiked-with-rage.html (accessed 18 October 2018.)

Schoenfeld, C. G. (1966) In Defense of Retribution in the Law. *The Psychoanalytic Quarterly*, 35: 108–121.

Shengold, L. (1994) Envy and Malignant Envy. *The Psychoanalytic Quarterly*, 63: 615–640.

Silver, J., Simons, A., and Craun, S. (2018) *A Study of the Pre-Attack Behaviors of Active Shooters in the United States 2000–2013*, Federal Bureau of Investigation, US Department of Justice, Washington DC 20535.

Sklar, J. (2011) Trauma, Psychosis, and Regression: the Psychoanalytic Treatment of a Schizophrenic Patient. In: *Landscapes of the Dark: History, Trauma and Psychoanalysis*. London: Karnac.

Sklar, J. (2019) *Dark Times: Psychoanalytic Perspectives on Politics, History and Mourning*. Bicester: Phoenix Publishing.

Socarides, S. W. (1966) On Vengeance – the Desire to 'Get Even'. *Journal of the American Psychoanalytic Association*, 14: 356–375.

Sopel, J. (2018) *If Only They Didn't Speak English: Notes from Trump's America*. London: BBC Books.

State of South Carolina (2016) *The State of South Carolina Plaintiff vs Jesse D Osborne Defendant: Transcript of Record, Interview of Jesse Osborne*, 28 September, 2016, County of Anderson, South Carolina.

Steiner, J. (1996) Revenge and Resentment in the 'Oedipus Situation'. *International Journal of Psycho-analysis*, 77: 433–443.

Steiner, J. (2015) Seeing and Being Seen: Shame in the Clinical Situation. *International Journal of Psycho-analysis*, 96: 1589–1601.

Stevenson, J. (2019) Hatred on the March. *New York Review of Books*. 21 November. Volume LXVI, No.18.

Strawson, P. F. (1974) *Freedom and Resentment and others essays*. Reprint, Abingdon: Routledge, 2008.

Suler, J. (2004) The Online Disinhibition Effect. *CyberPsychology and Behavior*, 7(3): 321–326.

Taylor, D. (2017) *Teenager jailed for trolling footballer Andy Woodward*. Available at: https://www.theguardian.com/uk-news/2017/dec/15/teenager-jailed-for-trolling-footballer-andy-woodward-about-abuse (accessed May 21 2019).

This American Life (2015): Radio show transcript of *545: If You Don't Have Anything Nice to Say, SAY IT IN ALL CAPS*. Available at: https://www.thisamericanlife.org/545/if-you-dont-have-anything-nice-to-say-say-it-in-all-caps) (accessed 18 June 2019).

Turk, V. (2018) *Meet the revenge porn lawyer working to put herself out of a job*. Available at: https://www.wired.co.uk/article/carrie-goldberg-sexual-privacy-revenge-porn-lawyer-interview (accessed 12 September 2019).

United States Court of Appeals First Circuit. United States of America, Appellee, v. Shawn Sayer, Defendant, Appellant. No. 12-2489. Decided May 2, 2014. Available at: https://law.justia.com/cases/federal/appellate-courts/ca1/12-2489/12-2489-2014-05-02.html (accessed 25 April 2019).

United States Department of Education Office for Civil Rights (2014) *Data Snapshot: School Discipline*. Issue Brief No. 1 (March 2014). Available at: https://ocrdata.ed.gov/Downloads/CRDC-School-Discipline-Snapshot.pdf (accessed 3 March 2019).

United States District Court, District of Kansas (Wichita Docket). United States of America, Plaintiff, v. Tyler R. Barriss, Shane M. Gaskill, and Casey S. Viner. Case no. 18-10065. Filed May 22, 2018. Available at: https://regmedia.co.uk/2018/05/24/barrissindictment.pdf (accessed 5 May 2019).

US Mass Shootings 1982–2018: Data from Mother Jones' Investigation. *Mother Jones.* Available at: https://www.motherjones.com/politics/2012/12/mass-shootings-mother-jones-full-data/ (accessed 12 September 2018).

US Secret Service and US Department of Education (June 2004) *The Final Report and Findings of the Safe School Initiative: Implications for the Prevention of School Attacks in the United States* (Washington, DC). Available at: https://rems.ed.gov/docs/FinalReportandFindingsofSafeSchoolInitiative.pdf (accessed 24 October 2018).

West, L. (2015) *What happened when I confronted my cruellest troll*. Available at: https://www.theguardian.com/society/2015/feb/02/what-happened-confronted-cruellest-troll-lindy-west (accessed 17 June 2019).

West, L. (2017) *Shrill: Notes from a Loud Woman*. London: Quercus.

Winnicott, D. W. (1939) Aggression and Its Roots. In: D. W. Winnicott *Deprivation and Delinquency* (2012) Abingdon: Routledge Classics.

Winnicott, D. W. (1957) On the Contribution of Direct Child Observation to Psychoanalysis. In: D. W. Winnicott *The Maturational Process and the Facilitating Environment*. Reprint, London: Karnac, 1990.

Winnicott, D. W. (1958) The Capacity to be Alone. In: D. W. Winnicott *The Maturational Process and the Facilitating Environment*. Reprint, London: Karnac, 1990.

Winnicott, D. W. (1960) The Theory of the Parent-Infant relationship. In: D. W. Winnicott *The Maturational Process and the Facilitating Environment*. Reprint, London: Karnac, 1990.

Winnicott, D. W. (1963a) From Dependence towards Independence in the Development of the Individual. In: D. W. Winnicott *The Maturational Processes and the Facilitating Environment*. Reprint, London: Karnac, 1990.

References

Winnicott, D. W. (1963b) Morals and Education. In: D. W. Winnicott *The Maturational Process and the Facilitating Environment*. Reprint, London: Karnac, 1990.

Winnicott, D. W. (1956) The Antisocial Tendency. In: D. W. Winnicott *Through Paediatrics to Psychoanalysis*. Reprint, London: Hogarth Press, 1992.

Winnicott, D. W. (1969) The Use of an Object. *International Journal of Psycho-analysis*, 50: 711–716.

Wood, H. (2011) The internet and its role in the escalation of sexually compulsive behaviour. *Psychoanalytic Psychotherapy*, 25(2): 127–142.

Woodward, A. (2019) *Position of Trust: A Football Dream Betrayed*. London: Coronet.

Wright, R, Topalli, V. and Jacques, S. (2017) Crime in Motion: Predation, Retaliation and the Spread of Urban Violence. In: B. Turner and G. Schlee (eds.) *On Retaliation*. New York: Berghahn.

Wurmser, L. (2015) Primary Shame, Mortal Wound and Tragic Circularity: Some New Reflections on Shame and Shame Conflicts. *International Journal of Psycho-analysis*, 96: 1615–1634.

Yorke, C. (1990) The development and functioning of the sense of shame. *Psychoanalytic Study of the Child*, 45: 377–409.

YouTube 28 July 2012: Hunter Moore interview. Available at: https://www.youtube.com/watch?v=h_1FIBA_kpk (accessed 22 June 2019).

YouTube 18 April 2018: Hunter Moore revenge porn king after prison interview. Available at: https://www.youtube.com/watch?v=Hzh9hUd9Of0 (accessed 22 June 2019).

Index

Index